ASK
LIKE A
LEADER

A METHOD FOR REVEALING DEEPER TRUTH AND TURNING BLIND SPOTS INTO BREAKTHROUGHS

LAUREN READY

Ask Like A Leader: A method for revealing deeper truth and turning
blindspots into breakthroughs
© Copyright 2025 Lauren Ready

For more information, email lauren@laurenready.com.

ISBN: 979-8-89694-816-2 - eBook

ISBN: 979-8-89694-817-9 - Paperback

GET YOUR FREE GIFT!

If you're like me, you might enjoy listening to a book while you read it. Which is exactly why I have recorded the audiobook and it's available for FREE to anyone who purchases a paperback version of *Ask Like A Leader*. Visit the page below and you'll also find a free downloadable version of the Question Lens™. Print it out. Post it on your desk. Share it with your team. Most importantly, use it in your next conversation. Having access to these resources will help you implement the methods in this book faster and take the next steps needed to lead with clarity.

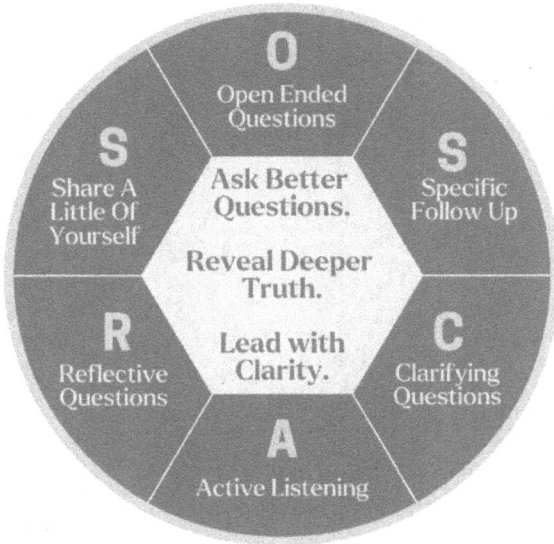

You can get a copy by visiting:
www.thequestionlens.com

To Scott: For always saying, "Go for it!" and never thinking a dream is too crazy to pursue. Thank you for being my greatest cheerleader, my best adventure partner, and my forever love.

To Max: You inspire me everyday. I am so grateful to be your mom. And I hope these words inspire you to lead with curiosity, no matter where life takes you.

To Mom & Dad: My lifelong supporters, encouragers, and inspiration. Thank you for modeling what hard work looks like, teaching me how to follow my passion, and showing us all what love and faith truly look like.

To Shannon: For always providing endless entertainment in the group chat, while also entertaining my ideas during our leadership chats. Thank you for cheering me on, even when it sounded a little crazy (and trying to take credit for … everything).

TABLE OF CONTENTS

**Part 3: Questions In Action: Living
and Leading With Curiosity**

THE POWER OF A FINAL QUESTION

"Is there anything else you'd like to add?"

That's the final question of virtually every interview I've ever conducted over the course of my career. I've asked it thousands of times. And so often, it results in something extraordinary. Most people follow with "no, but…"

The unseasonably cold April chill in Memphis started making me shiver as I wrapped up what had already been a thirty-minute on-camera interview with DeAndre, founder of a nonprofit that helped formerly incarcerated people. I had asked him everything, or so I thought. We had covered the mission of his organization, the impact of his work, and his personal journey of reentry into society after incarceration. My mind had already moved on to next steps: gathering footage, packing up the gear, and moving on to the edit.

As we were wrapping up, I casually asked that one final question: "Is there anything else you'd like to add?"

What happened next changed everything.

DeAndre paused, took a breath, and began to recite:

I am a success
I matter
I am important
I am somebody special
I am loved
I am needed
I am a positive role model
I am NOT my crime
I am NOT my past
I am new
God loves me
I love me
I will succeed!

That was the creed DeAndre wrote as a powerful self-affirmation. His voice was strong, until he realized (in that moment) the power of his own words. Then there was a crack in his voice as he realized his rallying cry was a declaration of identity and of transformation.

It's something he and program members say every single day at the end of each session together. Saying it together, in a safe place and as part of a community, was the essence of the organization's work. Sure, it was routine, but it was also a statement of belief in themselves, as individuals, and in each other.

The thing about that creed, and what I didn't know until I asked more questions, was that DeAndre wrote it from his prison cell. He was incarcerated for a crime he admitted to when it hit him: *I have the power to turn my life around and turn this experience into something positive for others.*

That moment of reflection birthed action. As he took pen to paper, he began to live out those words. And eventually, inspire others to do the same.

Back to our interview. As DeAndre recited the creed in front of my crew and me, I could see it land differently—even for him. Something he'd been saying every day, and inviting others to say too, took on a new weight. It was almost as if, in that moment, he truly recognized the impact his words had made.

And I realized something too: if I hadn't asked that final question, we would have missed it. We would have missed the emotional heartbeat of the film. He might never have reflected on the power of his own words. We wouldn't have discovered the title of our documentary: *You Must Believe: A LIFEline to Success.*[1]

After the film's release, that moment—DeAndre's words, his belief, and the power of his story—helped the documentary win a Regional Emmy Award, gain recognition at a local film festival, and become a powerful tool for DeAndre as he spoke to audiences across the country.

While DeAndre's story is more about his work and less about questions, it demonstrates the power of what questions can do for us and for others. In this book, we'll dive into how to do it better—to reveal deeper truths in all of us.

Back to the question. That simple invitation has a way of revealing what is true beneath what is prepared:

- A mother, asked if there is anything else to add, quietly hums the song she sings to her child every night. The piece stops being about services and starts being about love.

- In a community interview, a leader leans in and says the quiet part out loud. The best soundbite arrives after the cameras should have been off.

- In an interview with a lawyer after a teen signed a false confession to murder, we discovered we'll never know what happened in the room, because it wasn't recorded.

I have learned this again and again. The last question is not a throwaway. And neither is the first. That is what this book will teach you—ask on purpose and with purpose.

WHO THIS BOOK IS FOR

This book is for leaders—whether those leading a team, a business, or themselves.

It's for anyone who is an expert and sometimes feels the pressure to have all the answers.

It's for the new leader trying to navigate a new role with confidence and clarity (even when it doesn't feel certain).

It's for the seasoned leader looking to empower others.

It's for the solopreneur trying to figure out what life and business look like without someone holding them accountable.

I believe the most authentic way to connect isn't through having the right words—it's through asking the right questions. That's where the deeper truths come from, not from what we say, but from what we ask.

HOW THIS BOOK IS STRUCTURED

This book is divided into three parts, each building on the last to help you ask better questions and uncover deeper truths—in your leadership, your relationships, and yourself.

Part 1: The Curiosity Mindset: Why Questions Matter

We begin by exploring why curiosity is the foundation of great questions. You'll learn how expertise, certainty, and even familiarity can create blind spots—and how the right questions can reframe conversations, reveal hidden truths, and build stronger connections.

Part 2: The Question Lens™: A New Way to Focus

In this section, I'll introduce you to the Question Lens Method, a proven six-part method for asking better questions. Each chapter breaks down one essential type of question—Open-Ended, Specific Follow-Up, Clarifying, Active Listening, Reflective, and Share-A-Little—to help you sharpen your focus, deepen your conversations, and lead with clarity.

Part 3: Questions In Action: Living and Leading With Curiosity

Finally, we'll bring it all together. This part shows what it looks like to live and lead with curiosity in everyday life. You'll find stories, examples, and practices to help you make inquiry a habit—so you can use questions not just in high-stakes moments, but as a way of being.

Each chapter also includes a journal prompt with several questions for you to answer. I suggest you take 5–10 minutes to write your answers down and refer back to them as you continue reading the book. The questions are also great tools to use in weekly meetings, monthly one-on-ones or leadership retreats.

HOW TO USE THIS BOOK

I want to change the way you think about questions, not just as tools for getting answers, but as a way to unlock truths about your work, your team, your closest relationships, and even yourself. The right questions can shift perspectives, spark innovation, and build trust.

This book isn't about interrogation, it's about invitation. It's an invitation to lead with curiosity, to replace certainty with discovery, and to uncover the ideas, insights, and possibilities that live just beneath the surface.

Through stories from my work in journalism, filmmaking, leadership, and business, you'll see how powerful questions can reshape everything. Combined with a bit of science, psychology, and philosophy, I'll introduce you to the Question Lens™ method, a simple, practical approach to asking better questions. Each chapter includes:

- Stories that illustrate the impact of asking the right questions
- Reflection prompts to help you practice inquiry in your own life
- Tangible tools to shift from getting answers to leading with questions
- Journal prompts and space to answer

This isn't just a book to read, it's a book to use. Take the time to fill out the prompts and really consider how you can apply this book. Whether you're stepping into a high-stakes meeting, navigating a tough conversation, or trying to connect with someone new, use this guide to lead with curiosity and create meaningful change. When you ask better questions, you get better answers. More importantly, you uncover something greater: truth, trust, clarity, and possibility. Questions have power. The right ones can change the course of a conversation, a career, or even a life.

Which of these connect with you? Why do you want to ask
better questions?

Let's get started!

PART 1

THE CURIOSITY MINDSET: WHY QUESTIONS MATTER

CHAPTER 1

WHY WE STOP ASKING QUESTIONS — HOW EXPERTISE AND CERTAINTY STIFLE CURIOSITY

Do you consider yourself an expert in something? Maybe it's your career, a creative craft, or even yourself. Malcolm Gladwell popularized the idea that it takes 10,000 hours of deliberate practice to achieve mastery. He wrote in *Outliers*, "Practice isn't the thing you do once you're good. It's the thing you do that makes you good."[2]

I've always loved that idea, and, while it might be a bit oversimplified, there's solid research on the value of deliberate practice. Gladwell cites how the Beatles became the Beatles by performing more than 1,200 shows. They logged thousands of hours of repetition, mistakes, and refinement. Their rise wasn't magic. It was mastery.

But while I agree with the principle, I think it's important to add a caveat. *What happens after we become an expert?* Once we reach a certain level of skill or experience, there's a real risk we stop asking questions. That's when curiosity and innovation begin to fade.

Let's replace the word "expert" with titles like CEO, founder, team lead, director of development, or executive director. The more experience we gain, the fewer questions we tend to ask. It's not always done intentionally. Sometimes it's because we feel we should already know. Other times it's because we really do know a lot. But certainty has a side effect. It can cloud our curiosity.

I've seen it firsthand. The story I shared earlier about DeAndre and our documentary project proves how even seasoned experts, myself included, can almost forget to ask the questions that matter most. I'm not alone in this. Psychologists call it the "paradox of expertise."[3]

THE BLIND SPOTS OF BEING BRILLIANT

Here's the thing, expertise is often correct, but narrow. The very brain functions that make you good at something can also make you less open to what you don't already know.

Researchers at the University of Cambridge call this "paradoxical functional degradation." Essentially, the brain becomes so efficient that it stops noticing what it deems irrelevant.[4]

Let's break down three of the key trade-offs of expertise:

- Selective Attention: You become highly attuned to what you expect to see and filter out the rest. In a team meeting, this might look like catching the metrics, but missing someone's disengagement.

- Chunking: Your brain groups familiar information into mental shortcuts. This helps you move fast but also leads to assumptions about people, problems, or outcomes.

- Top-Down Processing: You rely on past knowledge to interpret the present. That's helpful, until a new variable throws off your instincts and you don't notice in time.

In medicine and forensic science, these patterns are well documented, but they also show up in leadership, sales, and team communication. If you've ever made a decision quickly and then realized later you missed something obvious, that's the paradox of expertise in action.[5]

And here's the kicker: The more skilled you become, the harder it is to notice that you've stopped noticing.

A MINDSET SHIFT: FROM "KNOWING" TO "NOTICING"

At the start of many of my keynotes, I ask participants to find something on them. Something in their pocket, bag, or on their body that tells a story no one at their table knows. It could be a photo, a piece of jewelry, a receipt, or a keychain. The introverts cringe. The extroverts light up. But something magical happens every time.

"This ring was my grandmother's. I wear it every day to remind me she's with me."

"This is my national park pass. I'm trying to visit them all with my family."

"This notebook has my daily gratitude list. It keeps me grounded."

These aren't polished stories, they're real ones. These objects are ordinary to the person, but extraordinary to the listener. As each story unfolds, the room softens. People sit up. They listen more closely. They get curious.

And just like that, we've shifted from assuming we know people to realizing we don't, from certainty to inquiry.

This simple exercise reminds us what happens when we lead with questions instead of answers. It opens up connections. It surfaces the truth. It builds trust.

You can do this at your next staff meeting or company retreat. Ask your team to tell a story about an object they have with them. See what unfolds. Because every time you shift from "I already know" to "What don't I know yet?" you invite insight.

FOR THE YOUNG LEADER: THE NOT-YET EXPERT

If you're early in your career, new to leadership, or just new to your role, you might feel the opposite pull. You don't have all the answers, but it feels like you should, especially if you've just been promoted or trusted with a big responsibility.

Let me say this clearly. You don't need to know everything to be effective. You need to stay curious.

Here are a few mindset reframes and question prompts that can help:

- Instead of feeling pressure to impress, ask: "What can I learn from the people in this room?"

- Instead of faking certainty, say: "That's a great question. I don't have the full picture yet, but I'd love to dig in with you."

- Instead of seeing your lack of experience as a liability, remember: New eyes often see what seasoned ones miss. Use your fresh perspective as an asset.

- Keep a curiosity mantra. Try: "I'm here to ask better questions, not prove I have the answers."

This played out right in front of me when I watched one of my newer team members stay completely silent during a project kickoff meeting. Later, she told me she hadn't spoken up because she didn't want to seem naive or out of place—and she definitely didn't want to step on anyone's toes. At the same time, I felt pressure—not to prove I was the visionary leader with all the answers, but to be that leader.

It turns out, that's a terrible combination: a team member afraid to ask anything, and a leader who thinks they have to know everything. What we both needed was curiosity. When I finally acknowledged that I didn't have it all figured out, it opened the door for her to speak up. Her perspective ended up shaping the direction of our project in a meaningful way. That's the power of letting go of certainty—on both sides of the table.

JOURNAL PROMPT

Before you turn the page, pause. The patterns you've just read about—selective attention, chunking, top-down processing—aren't abstract ideas. They're already shaping the way you lead, listen, and decide.

Think of a time when you *assumed* you already knew the answer. What question could you have asked instead that might have revealed something new?

- Where in your work or life are you most confident? How might that confidence be creating blind spots?

- Recall a moment when someone surprised you with their perspective. What made you open to hearing it?

- If you replaced "I already know" with "What don't I know yet?" in one conversation this week, what might change?

These questions are your chance to slow down, notice where certainty might be closing a door, and invite curiosity back in.

CHAPTER 2

BREAKING THE ASSUMPTION CYCLE — HOW TO CHALLENGE BIASES THROUGH INQUIRY

You know that saying, "When you assume, you make an ass out of you and me." You assume a lot more than you realize, especially with the people you know best.

It's likely one of the most ironic communication traps you fall into: The closer you are to someone, the more likely you are to overestimate how well you understand each other. You'd think shared history and mutual trust would improve communication, but in many cases, it does the opposite.

And there's science to prove it! It's a phenomenon known as "closeness-communication bias," a concept explored by psychologists Kenneth Savitsky (Williams College) and Boaz Keysar (University of Chicago). Their research shows that people often communicate less clearly with close friends, spouses, or colleagues than they do with strangers, simply because they assume they "just know" what they mean.[6]

Raise your hand if this has happened to you? I have both hands up!

Closeness breeds confidence. Confidence leads to shortcuts. Shortcuts skip curiosity. But closeness-communication bias doesn't operate in a vacuum. It's tangled up with other biases too:

- **Confirmation Bias:** You seek out interpretations that match what you already believe, and often ask questions to validate your bias.

- **Availability Heuristic:** You rely on what comes to mind first, instead of reflecting on what is true.

- **Egocentrism:** You believe your thoughts are more transparent than they are, so you go on assuming others can "just tell" what you mean.

- **Recency Bias:** You just went through this with another employee or customer. You feel there's a trend here, so you should treat this the same as that one, instead of as a new, unique situation.

Together, these cognitive blind spots create an assumption cycle that can derail even the best relationships and teams.

THE ILLUSION OF BEING UNDERSTOOD

In one of Savitsky and Keysar's most cited studies[6], participants were asked to interpret ambiguous phrases, and give instructions to either a friend or a stranger. Across multiple experiments, people believed they would be more easily understood by friends, yet the actual success rates were no better than with strangers. In some cases, miscommunication was even worse with close connections.[7]

Think of a time you were certain someone close to you understood your message, but they didn't. What happened? How did your assumptions play a role in the miscommunication? Did you recognize it in the moment or only in hindsight?

I remember once working with a team member I really trusted. We'd collaborated for years, had great rhythm, and finished each other's sentences more often than not. So when I said, "It'd be great to have that draft done soon," I assumed we were on the same page.

In my head, "soon" meant the end of the day tomorrow. In their head, "soon" meant sometime next week.

When that draft didn't come by the next day, I felt the tension rise. I started writing the rest of the conversation in my head, you know, the passive-aggressive kind with a fake-friendly, "Just checking in!" and a timestamp that said, "I was expecting this already." But I caught myself. I hadn't actually communicated a deadline. I'd let the comfort of familiarity become a shortcut, and the clarity got lost.

That's closeness bias at work: when we assume shared understanding, and skip the very questions that create it.

Now I try to pause and ask: "What does 'soon' look like on your calendar?" It's a small question that saves a lot of cleanup later.

At home, this happens even more often, especially with my husband. We've been together long enough that I often start a sentence with, "Hey, can you handle that thing?" and expect him to read my mind. And often he does. But that makes the misses even harder to spot. It should also be noted that at the time of writing this book, we work together every single day, running our video production company and raising our elementary-school-aged son, Max. So we might be the definition of closeness communication bias.

One time, before a family trip, I asked him to "take care of packing for Max." He nodded. I moved on. In my mind, that meant clothes, toothbrush, books for the drive, and the stuffed animal Max couldn't sleep without.

When we were halfway to our destination, Max asked for his bedtime stuffie. I looked at Scott, and Scott looked at me. No stuffie.

He said, "You just said pack his stuff. I thought you meant clothes."

And he wasn't wrong. I had assumed, because we know each other so well, that he'd know *exactly* what I meant. But I didn't actually say it. We were both operating on different interpretations of the same vague instruction.

What did I learn? Even the people we know best can't read our minds (thank god!). And expecting them to read our minds can create frustration that curiosity could've prevented.

Now I've learned to ask: "Want me to clarify what I'm picturing?" or "Should we make a checklist?" It's a little question that opens the door to better teamwork, whether it's packing for a trip or planning a video shoot. And for the record, I'm more guilty of not packing the stuffie than he is!

Closeness-communication bias isn't just an academic idea. It plays out constantly in our lives.

- **In partnerships**: One partner says, "You know what I mean," but the other really doesn't. Frustration follows.

- **At work**: A leader skips details in a conversation with their longtime team member, assuming alignment, but the results miss the mark.

- **Among friends**: A casual "I'm fine" goes unquestioned, even when it's clearly not fine, because we don't want to offend or assume too much.

Think about the last time this happened to you. Was it with a partner? A trusted colleague? A longtime friend? We often don't realize we've assumed something until the tension hits.

But every assumption is an opportunity to pause, rewind, and ask the question we skipped. That's how you turn a moment of miscommunication into a moment of connection.

WHY INQUIRY MATTERS

To break this bias, we need to shift from assumption to inquiry. Curiosity becomes the tool that disrupts our overconfidence and invites clarity. We don't need to interrogate. We just need to ask.

Instead of:

- "They already know this," try, "What's your understanding of this?"
- "They're probably thinking what I'm thinking," try, "What's your take on it?"
- "They nodded confidently, so they must agree," try, "What is missing here?"

It sounds simple. But it can change everything.

For example, I once walked out of a meeting with a client, feeling confident. The conversation was smooth, they nodded at the right places, and when I wrapped up the plan, they said, "Sounds good."

Check, check, check. Or so I thought.

Some time later, when I sent the deliverables, I got a polite but surprising reply: "Thanks for this, but this isn't quite what we were envisioning. Can we hop on a call to regroup?"

Cue the gut-drop moment.

I went back and replayed the meeting in my mind. They hadn't objected. They hadn't asked many questions. Now I realized, they also hadn't really said *yes* in a clear, enthusiastic way. I had filled in the silence with my own assumptions, thinking our closeness and prior rapport meant alignment.

Here's the part that stung a little more: I saw it all *so clearly* in my own mind. As a creative, when I get that initial spark— the vision, the concept, the structure—I can almost see the finished piece before it exists. It's vivid. It's layered. It makes perfect sense *to me*.

Here's the trap: What's clear in my head doesn't always translate through words alone. Especially when I assume others can see it too. Without taking time to invite their perspective, to ask, "What are you picturing?" or "How does this match the story you're trying to tell?" I risk misalignment, even with the best intentions.

That's closeness bias. That's the assumption cycle.

Now, I build more space into conversations for curiosity. I ask questions about painpoints, obstacles, and who might need to give feedback and insight before I even begin, even when things feel "fine."

Silence isn't always agreement and nodding doesn't always mean clarity.

MAKE THE FAMILIAR STRANGE

One powerful tool for breaking the assumption cycle is to approach familiar conversations as if you're speaking to a stranger. Not in formality, but in *thoughtfulness*.

Think about how carefully you explain something to someone brand new. You pause. You give context. You ask questions like, "What questions do you have?" or "Am I missing anything?" You don't skip steps or speak in shorthand.

Now think about how you talk to people you know really well. The shorthand gets shorter. The questions fade away. The assumptions take over. I've learned, sometimes the hard way, that it pays to bring that thoughtful energy into even the most everyday conversations, especially with the people closest to you.

For example, every Sunday night, my husband and I have a family meeting. We live and work together, so this is the whole picture of the week, business and personal. We map out the week ahead—school drop-offs, video shoots, travel, meetings, and all the puzzle pieces of two business owners raising a kid. On one of those nights, Scott said, "We should be fine if you take Max to school Thursday." Normally, I would've just nodded and moved on. But something about the phrasing—*"should be fine if…"*—felt vague.

Instead of assuming we were aligned, I asked, "What do you mean by *should be fine*? Do you need me to take him, or are you just saying you're available if I can't?"

"I have a meeting—I need you to take him," he responded.

That one clarifying question saved us both from a stressful Thursday morning. As it turned out, he had a tight client call and was hoping I could take Max. He could make it work, so he didn't come out and say it directly. I could easily accommodate it, and now we were on the same page.

It was a small moment—but a reminder that when the people closest to you say something familiar, it's still worth pausing to clarify what they really mean. Making the familiar strange doesn't require overthinking. Just curiosity.

That's the danger of the familiar. You skip the questions. You assume alignment. And sometimes, you build entire days (or projects) around something that's not even real.

So now, instead of saying, "We should be good," I ask, "Can we go over this together and see if it works on your end?" It takes two extra minutes. But it saves lots of scrambling.

Consider a recent miscommunication you had with someone you know well (a spouse, a colleague, a close friend).

- What caused the miscommunication?
- If you could go back and redo that moment, how would you incorporate more curiosity? How could that have brought clarity?
- What can you do this week to communicate with more curiosity and less certainty?

Closeness doesn't earn a shortcut, it demands curiosity. The people you know best still deserve your best questions. The more you slow down and ask, the more you invite understanding, trust, and ironically, true efficiency.

Assumptions feel fast. But questions get you there faster.

CHAPTER 3

A PERSONAL STORY — THE ROLE OF CURIOSITY IN JOURNALISM

Curiosity has always been my compass. Long before I created frameworks or delivered keynotes, I was a teenage production assistant in a newsroom—watching reporters chase breaking stories and ask bold questions. Looking back, that early training in journalism didn't just teach me how to tell stories—it taught me how to ask the right questions. And those questions changed everything: my career, my business, my leadership, and my life.

This chapter isn't just about my story. It's about how following your questions—even the uncomfortable ones—can lead you to your next chapter. Because sometimes the most important questions aren't the ones we ask of others. They're the ones we ask ourselves.

A START IN THE NEWSROOM

I was sixteen years old when I stepped into a newsroom for the first time. A meteorologist from my church invited me to job shadow at the local ABC affiliate in Cedar Rapids, Iowa. The urgency of the newsroom—the energy, the purpose—hooked me instantly.

By seventeen, I applied for a job there. I knew it was a long shot, but I asked myself: What have I got to lose? After a short interview, I was hired as a production assistant—the youngest on staff. My job included moving, aligning, and setting cameras, sorting scripts, and sprinting up two flights of stairs to physically deliver last-minute beta tapes to master control. Every second mattered.

After school, I'd head straight to the station and stay through the 10:00 p.m. newscast. In between shows, I watched editors cut news packages, reporters pitch ideas, and heard journalists call sources—all asking bold, curious questions. I didn't know it then, but that job would shape everything about who I am and how I lead. It taught me that asking better questions reveals better stories.

Curiosity was the fuel of journalism. It drove reporters to dig deeper, ask again, and look beyond the obvious. When I became a full-time reporter, I learned that the best stories weren't just about facts—they were about finding the heartbeat underneath.

Whether I was covering a marching band attending the inauguration of President Obama, the aftermath of deadly tornadoes in Oklahoma, or protests in Ferguson, Missouri, the difference between a good story and a great one was always the same: *the depth of the questions.*

A MOMENT OF FORGIVENESS IN A JUVENILE COURT HALLWAY

Before I ever taught others how to ask better questions, I was the one holding the microphone. For more than a decade, I worked as a television journalist—chasing storms, covering presidents, standing on the front lines of protests and parades alike. But it wasn't the chaos or the spectacle that shaped me the most. It was quiet, unexpected moments—like one in a juvenile court hallway.

One of the most powerful moments in my journalism career didn't happen on camera.

I was covering the sentencing hearing of a teen involved in a violent grocery store assault that had gone viral. Cameras weren't allowed in the courtroom. I felt stuck. My job was to *show* the story. How could I do that without visuals?

Inside the courtroom, emotions ran high. The teenage suspect admitted he attacked a worker to impress a girl. The victim, still suffering from PTSD, described how he relived the moment every day. When court adjourned, the families spilled into the hallway—and something extraordinary happened.

The suspect's mother turned to the victim's father: "I'm so sorry for what my son did, and I wish he was here to apologize himself."

The father leaned toward the suspect's mother and replied, "Tell your son I forgive him."

No cameras. No recordings. Just raw, human grace and forgiveness.

The official story barely mentioned it—just one sentence, preceded by the tabloid-like testimony. But when I shared it in my own words on Facebook, the response was overwhelming. It reminded me that asking the right questions can reveal something deeper—not just information, but transformation.

Of course, it also forced me to ask myself a question: What story are you telling—and is there a deeper one underneath?

That moment sparked a new line of inquiry in me:

- *What story should I be telling here?*
- *What's beyond the headline?*
- *What's the story that will move people to act? Rather than just scare them?*

That hallway moment was the beginning of my exit from TV news. Over the next 18 months, I kept asking harder questions:

- *How could I leave my dream job?*

- *Could I build a business telling the stories that mattered to me?*
- *Would people still care if they didn't see it on the evening news?*

In March 2016, I declined to renew my contract and walked away from my career in broadcast journalism. I left a job I had worked years to land—in a top 50 market—to chase something I couldn't fully explain yet. I didn't know how it would turn out, but curiosity pulled me forward.

In my first 10 months as a full-time business owner, I was able to tell so many stories of impact. I hit six figures in revenue working solo. I was proud. And exhausted. When the calendar flipped to January 2017, reality hit: There were no guarantees. I started back at zero.

That sparked another round of questions:

- *Can I keep up this pace?*
- *What would it take to hire help?*
- *Do I even know how to hire?*

The answers didn't come quickly. But I followed the questions. I wrote a job description. Conducted interviews. And hired my first employee.

Where is your curiosity nudging you to go next—and what would happen if you followed it?

CURIOSITY AS A LEADERSHIP SKILL

What started as a chance to take a bit of a load off me, led to steady growth and hiring for the next five years. We were growing faster than I could keep up—outgrowing office spaces, gear capacity, and technology. It was really fun! And also really hard. I didn't have the skills I needed to lead and invest in a team, share my vision, and grow the company. I asked myself:

- What do I need to learn?
- How can I build myself into a better leader?
- What do other business owners do to grow and lead?
- Is there a place where I can talk about money challenges, people challenges, and personal challenges without judgement?
- Can I grow with a group of people who will also hold me accountable to making the right choices?

That's how I found Vistage, including a coach and a peer network of small business owners. Each month, we meet to share challenges, learn together, and get coached. This group became my curiosity lab. I didn't just learn how to run a better business. I learned how to ask better questions of my team—and of myself.

I can tell you, I haven't been a perfect leader, and you'll continue to hear some of my woes in this book.

Curiosity has helped me:

- Build a culture of trust
- Invite ideas instead of dictate direction
- Empower team members to grow and lead
- Recognize my blind spots
- Lead with clarity and connection

And let me be clear: I'm still learning. I've made mistakes. I've been the leader who didn't listen closely enough. But every time I've paused to ask a better question, the path forward became clearer.

Curiosity isn't just for collecting information—it's for transformation. The right question can reveal the real story, unlock a new direction, or help you see what's been in front of you all along.

Reflect on your own path:

- What can curiosity reveal to you about your current role, project, or team?
- What hard question have you been avoiding?
- What might shift if you asked it?

Leadership isn't about having all the answers. It's about asking the questions that move you—and your people—forward.

So I challenge you: Where in your life or leadership do you need to ask a better question?

CHAPTER 4

THE COST OF NOT ASKING — MISSED OPPORTUNITIES AND STAGNATION

Imagine if I hadn't asked myself the right questions about my career path. I most certainly wouldn't have taken a leap to build my own business.

A few weeks into my new venture, a friend asked me: *What's a story you always wanted to tell but couldn't in the newsroom?*

I knew the answer immediately: The Carpenter Art Garden Bike Shop. It was a place teaching kids about bike repair and offering life lessons along the way. I became familiar with it because I was frequently in the area covering crime. But the Carpenter Art Garden and Bike Shop were affecting real change. It was the kind of story I'd always wanted to explore more deeply.

As I began filming, I intended to focus on the students—track their success through the program. How could these kids' trajectory be changed by learning these skills? But that isn't what happened. The reality of the challenges in the kids' lives proved overwhelming. My naivety to the true obstacles caused my preconceived narrative to fall apart. The project was at risk.

As my hope in the story began to fade, I asked a familiar question: *What other story should I be telling here?*

And that's when I turned the camera toward the mentor, Lee Evans. He grew up in the neighborhood, knew the struggle, and had become a mentor to the next generation. Our interview revealed something deeper:

> **LEE:** It's harder to do right than wrong, when wrong is all around them. You know, the bike is the first car for a young man. So if he wants to keep his car running, he's gotta come to the shop, and in the midst of working on his car, we work on his life.

> **LEE:** For me, every day is like a new day. My life is constantly changing. I had to realize that it was changing, accept the change, and then explain to them why I'm changing, so they can feel better about changing.

The story became about Lee finding purpose, mentorship, and personal growth. It wasn't about a bike program or the kids anymore—it was about his own human transformation. And that story went on to be nominated and win an Emmy—my first. It was a dream I had released when I exited the television news business.

What dream have you quietly set aside, assuming it's no longer relevant? What question might bring it back to life?

This one had two risks, Lee's story not being told and, it turned out, a long-sought industry recognition. This story isn't just for journalists or creatives. It's a universal reminder: When your plans start to unravel, curiosity is often the way back to clarity. Asking a better question can rescue an opportunity that's on the edge of being missed.

DREAMS AND INSTINCT

Not all questions lead to happy, dream-fulfilling answers. But they can lead to the *right* answers anyway.

Sometimes I don't ask the question. In fact, I *avoid* asking the question because I know the answer isn't great. Avoidance is one of my saboteurs. Often it's because I want to be liked, but usually I don't want to face the hard thing in front of me. Avoidance often hits at times when I know I need to take action.

In spring of 2025, I was nearly a year into opening a new location of our office. We had been "on the ground" for twelve months and had two committed team members. Eighteen months prior, I had a dream of opening another Midwest location, close to family, in a place that felt a lot like our home office. I assumed that if I hired the right people, we could make it happen.

The team was value-aligned and growing in the things that mattered most: getting results for our clients. We got great results, but didn't have enough clients. The sales volume just wasn't coming in. In fact, at the time of this difficult decision, we were nearly $60,000 in the red with only a small percentage of that in the project pipeline. My dream of thriving in another market wasn't playing out like I envisioned, and it wasn't entirely my team's fault.

Sure, there were parts of the economic landscape and current events that were preventing sales success. I should have done more "on the ground" work to help build a stronger presence. I should have coached my team better about what to do in certain situations and how to cultivate new clients. I put trust in them, but trust wasn't the issue.

They needed my leadership and experience. I had two other offices, was pursuing two documentary projects, raising a six-year-old, and trying to be a good wife and partner. The team was bought in. They believed in the mission. And we were getting meetings and sending proposals. When we won a project, we did excellent work on it. But I didn't ask the clarifying questions to go deeper. Why were we missing on so many proposals? What was missing from the close? Were we communicating a vision and establishing trust? It's probably a mix, but I wasn't asking clearly enough to know.

I kept pretending like it would get better, hoping and wishing some big project would come through. I was losing sleep over it and avoiding the conversation that really needed to be had.

Then, one day I was driving to work and listening to *Meditations for Mortals* by Oliver Burkeman when I heard a quote from Sheldon B. Kopp: "You are free to do whatever you'd like. You need only face the consequences."[8]

What were the consequences of not taking action? What was the cost of continuing to wish and hope we'd see a change? And what harm would I eventually cause to everyone in the company if I didn't have a hard conversation?

It was through asking questions of myself and my business that I realized it was time to take action, but it didn't happen overnight. There were multiple meetings, tough conversations, and moments of deep reflection. We asked hard questions of ourselves, our team, and the situation itself.

Can we meet this goal? What would it look like to pursue one of these three paths? Is there a version of this business model that doesn't result in operating at a loss? What are we holding onto? Was the plan good but just slow developing? Was the plan naive? Were the initial assumptions just wrong?

These weren't theoretical questions. They were pointed, practical, and at times, painful. And in those meetings, as honest answers started to surface, the reality became clearer: We needed to change course. There was no realistic path to breakeven, let alone profit. We had done good work. We had good people. But good intentions couldn't cover the cost of staying the same. We had to close the location completely.

This one still hurts. I really wanted it to work. Letting go is never easy, especially when it involves people you care about and dreams you once believed would thrive. And yet, I know that choice was a catalyst, for all of us. A return to focus, alignment, process, and supporting the team.

THE INSTINCT FILTER

If you'd like to avoid the optimism trap or you want to test your instinct, I suggest using what I call the instinct filter. When you're facing a moment of doubt or indecision, use this simple three-part filter:

1. Is this discomfort rooted in fear or in fact?

2. Is my instinct to avoid, delay, or diminish the truth?

3. What might change if I got curious instead of staying comfortable?

We often assume that our instincts are always right, but unexamined instinct can mask avoidance. Thinking about these questions through a curiosity lens will truly help you test your instinct with reality.

Application Prompt: Think about a recent decision you made—or avoided. Run it through the instinct filter. What did you learn?

Sometimes asking a question prevents a missed opportunity. Other times, it forces us to make a hard but necessary choice. Either way, curiosity clears the fog.

So back to you:

- What's something you should be asking right now?
- How would asking that question prevent a missed opportunity?
- How might it move you from stagnant to courageous action?

The longer we avoid asking the question, the greater the risk— not just of failure, but of missing the clarity we need to grow.

Where are you being invited to get curious—even if it's uncomfortable?

CHAPTER 5

CURIOSITY VS. JUDGMENT — THE MINDSET SHIFT THAT MAKES ALL THE DIFFERENCE

"Be curious, not judgmental." That quote is forever misattributed to Walt Whitman. The earliest known appearance actually traces back to a 1986 advice column by Marguerite and Marshall Shearer. Still, it found new life through the Apple TV series *Ted Lasso*—and that's where it hit home for me.

I've watched *Ted Lasso* more times than I'd like to admit. There are so many leadership lessons embedded in the show, especially in how Ted himself leads—with empathy, humor, and an unwavering sense of curiosity.[9]

One of the most memorable scenes happens in Season 1, Episode 8, during a high-stakes game of darts. Ted delivers a monologue about the difference between judgment and curiosity:[9]

> "All them fellas who used to belittle me, none of them were curious. They thought they had everything figured out. So they judged everything and everyone. If they were curious, they would've asked questions. Like, 'Have you played a lot of darts, Ted?'"

As it turns out, Ted had—every Sunday with his dad until he passed away.

"If they were curious, they would've asked more questions."

That one line stuck with me. Because the same is true in leadership. When we lead with judgment, we close off connections. When we lead with curiosity, we open the door to understanding.

When I first saw that scene, I saw it through the lens of being underestimated. But the more I reflected, the more I realized, I've also been the one who judged too quickly—without asking questions.

One moment stands out. I had what I assumed would be a simple conversation with a team member. I asked them to join me for an important shoot on a Saturday evening. Their response was hesitant: "I don't think I can do that."

Immediately, I made a snap judgment. *They're not committed. They're not a team player. They don't care as much as I do. I'm so flexible with them yet they're not reciprocating that at all.*

But I never asked why. I didn't offer space for a conversation. I just shifted the conversation and asked another team member. I was still clearly annoyed and angry and it probably showed. Later, I learned their family was visiting from out of town. They wanted to help—but I hadn't given them enough context or time to rearrange their plans.

Had I led with curiosity instead of judgment, I would have asked:

- "What's holding you back from saying yes?"
- "Is there flexibility that would make this work for both of us?"

I didn't ask. And I missed an opportunity to build trust.

WHEN JUDGMENT GETS IN THE WAY

Judgment shuts doors. Curiosity opens them. They can't exist in the same moment. Let's look at the contrast more closely.

When we lead with judgment, we:

- Assume we already know
- Jump to conclusions
- Label others
- Shut the door on connection

When we lead with curiosity, we:

- Pause to consider what we don't know yet
- Give our team members a chance to shine
- Open ourselves to new possibilities
- Ask questions that build trust and understanding

Let me show you what this looked like in real time for a colleague of mine.

She was leading a team meeting when another team member challenged one of her decisions. Her first instinct was to defend her stance. She had the experience, she was the leader. But she caught herself. She paused and asked, "Can you help me understand what you're seeing that I might be missing?"

That single question changed the energy in the room. The team member shared a new perspective that highlighted a risk no one had considered. That insight shaped the final decision—and deepened the trust on the team.

That's the difference. Judgment ends the conversation. Curiosity keeps it going.

In fact, curiosity isn't passive. It's active, intentional, and brave. It's a decision to stay open when your brain wants to shut down or shut someone out.

The next time you feel yourself making a snap judgment, pause and ask, "What else could be true?"

NOTICE AND ACT

Before moving on to the next step of this book, pause here and put curiosity into practice. This shift has to happen before you can ask better questions using the Question Lens™.

Here's a three-step exercise to flip your mindset:

1. *Notice your mental autopilot.* This week, pay attention to how often your first reaction is a judgment. Write down three moments where you could have responded with curiosity instead.

2. Use this reframe. When someone frustrates you, silently ask:

   o "I wonder what they're protecting."

   o "I wonder what story they're living."

   o "What don't I know yet?"

3. Ask. Follow up. Ask the questions that come to mind. (In the next chapter, I'll walk you through the exact framework I use to ask better questions.)

This is what it looks like to go from knowing to noticing. And noticing is a powerful tool.

- When was the last time I made a wrong assumption that changed once I asked a question?

- How does judgment show up in my leadership style?

- What does it feel like, physically and emotionally, when I choose curiosity over control?

This shift from judging to wondering is more than a mindset tweak. It's a gateway to deeper connection and better outcomes.

Now that you've learned to choose curiosity, we'll go one step further. In the next section, I'll introduce the Question Lens™ method and the OSCARS framework, a tool to help you frame questions in a way that invites, rather than intimidates. Because it's not just *what* you ask, it's *how* you ask.

PART 2

THE QUESTION LENS™: A NEW WAY TO FOCUS

CHAPTER 6

INTRODUCTION TO THE QUESTIONS LENS™

Before we dive into the individual chapters that break down the Question Lens™, I want to pause and offer you the full view, the big picture behind why this model matters and how it works.

The Question Lens™ is more than just a list of better questions. It's a way to zoom in on truth, focus conversations, and reveal the details that would otherwise be missed. It's a method. A mindset. A magnifying lens for leadership, connection, and change.

Imagine a camera lens. At first, the image is blurry. You think you see what's in front of you, but something's missing. It's vague, out of focus.

That's what happens when we lead with assumptions or rush through conversations. We think we know what someone is trying to say. We think we understand the problem. But until we slow down and adjust the lens, we risk missing what matters most. When we slow down, things come into focus and we begin to lead with clarity.

Each part of the Question Lens™ spells the word OSCARS and should be thought of like a click of the focus ring on a camera. Each part is a subtle shift that sharpens the image.

The Question Lens™ – Lens Adjustments for Leaders		
Lens Adjustment	What You're Doing	What It Unlocks
O – Open-Ended Questions	Start the inquiry	Spark insight
S – Specific Follow-Up	Dig into what matters	Go deeper
C – Clarifying Questions	Clear misunderstandings	Reveal true meaning
A – Active Listening	Fully engage	Hear what's unspoken
R – Reflection Questions	Encourage pause and process	Inspire growth
S – Share a Little	Build reciprocal trust	Deepen connection

When used together, these elements guide you from assumption to awareness, from noise to nuance, from surface-level conversation to meaningful exchange.

The result? You lead with more confidence, more clarity, and more connection. You see the full picture—sharp, true, and focused. This is the heart of the Question Lens™.

In the next chapters, we'll zoom in on each of these elements through stories, tools, and prompts. I invite you to hold this image in your mind as we go: a blurry scene slowly sharpening into focus, click by click, question by question.

Let's focus.

CHAPTER 7

OPEN-ENDED QUESTIONS — WHY "YES" OR "NO" ISN'T ENOUGH

It was clear something wasn't quite right.

We were sitting one-on-one, and while the conversation started with updates and project check-ins, the energy just wasn't there. This employee who was smart, capable, usually upbeat seemed withdrawn. Less engaged. Less fulfilled. A recent change in our operations had stirred up some emotions. We were redrafting everyone's job titles and roles and attempting to give everyone a path for growth, but our conversation wasn't leading to any growth. I could feel the weight of it in the room.

At that moment, I had two choices. I could lead with my own assumptions:

- Are you unhappy with your role?
- Are the changes frustrating you?
- Do you even want to be here?

All yes-or-no questions. All based on *my* interpretation of what might be going on.

But instead, I asked, "What's your dream? What do you really want to do?"

That question changed everything. Part of the reason I asked it was because I remembered a time when I was the one sitting on the other side of the table.

Years ago, a manager had asked me the same thing: "What's your dream? Where do you see yourself in five years?"

But I didn't tell the truth. I wasn't sure if it was safe. I didn't know if saying it out loud would hurt my chances of getting promoted or make me seem disloyal. So I gave the safe answer: "I want to be an investigative journalist here in this newsroom."

I didn't even believe myself when I said it.

What I really wanted? To start my own business. One that would help nonprofits tell their stories through video. One that would empower people to work toward something meaningful instead of leading from fear.

So when I asked that question during a one-on-one with my team member, I didn't just ask it to gather information. I asked it to create space in a judgment-free, safe place.

That question, coupled with the open question culture in our office, led to hearing the truth. They said, "I want to start my own business."

From there, showing support and continuing to make it safe, the next open-ended question came naturally: "What's it going to take to make that happen?"

We then worked together to get them there. Progressively, collaboratively, and in a way that worked for both of us.

Open-ended questions don't just gather facts. They *invite truth*. They *signal trust*. They say, "I'm not here to steer you, I'm here to understand you."

Open-ended questions do more than invite conversation, they activate the brain in ways that foster deeper thinking and connection.

When someone hears a yes-or-no question, their brain quickly scans for a binary answer. But when you ask an open-ended question, you engage their prefrontal cortex, the part of the brain responsible for higher-order thinking, problem-solving, and reflection. This cognitive shift taps into a strategy known as *elaborative interrogation*, which helps people connect new information to what they already know. It boosts comprehension and leads to deeper insights.[10]

And because open-ended questions feel less judgmental, they foster psychological safety. That safety shifts the brain from a defensive posture into one of curiosity and connection.[11]

LEADERSHIP AND LOADED QUESTIONS

That's why questions matter so much, especially in leadership. We often walk into conversations with a goal in mind: resolve the tension, retain the employee, fix the performance issue. Because of that, our questions become loaded. We ask things like, "Are you feeling frustrated with the new structure?" or "Is this still a good fit for you?" Yes-or-no prompts that subtly point toward the answer we think we are going to hear. The question is *loaded* with assumption and judgment. We may as well ask, "Can you confirm what I already know?" That is not trust nor leadership.

Open-ended questions shift the focus from *our* agenda to *their* reality. They sound like:

- "What do you want more of in your work right now?"
- "What's getting in the way?"
- "If you could design your ideal role, what would it look like?"
- "What's your dream?"

When asked with real curiosity, not manipulation or strategy, they reveal things we can't plan for: fears, longings, ideas that never felt safe to share. They don't just help us solve a problem. They help us see the whole person.

This only can work if we get comfortable with not knowing the answer in the moment. The team member might (and probably will) say something completely unexpected. If we need to already know the tactical response, that's not curiosity.

That's what happened in that one-on-one. Because I was willing to ask a question I didn't know the answer to, I learned something that changed the direction of our work together. And more importantly, I helped someone move one step closer to their dream and one step closer to their purpose and their truth.

SIMPLE TRICK: INTERVIEWING A KID

If all of this still feels a little abstract, here's a simple way I used to think about it back when I worked in the news: When you're interviewing a child, if you only ask yes-or-no questions, that's exactly what you'll get: yes or no. The key is to challenge yourself to ask something open-ended enough that even a child has the space to respond with more.

That same idea applies to all of us. When you frame your questions in a way that makes people feel safe, seen, and curious, you're giving them permission to go deeper. And when you keep it simple, like you're talking to a kid, it suddenly doesn't feel so intimidating.

Open-ended questions aren't just a communication technique. They're an invitation to depth. They create space for clarity, for connection, and for change. When we stop asking questions that lead to the answer we *want*, and start asking questions that lead to the *truth*, we not only grow as leaders, we grow the people around us.

And when used in conjunction with the rest of the Question Lens™, open-ended questions are just the beginning. They crack the door open. What comes next, specific follow-ups, clarifying questions, active listening, reflection, and sharing can reveal so much more than we ever expected.

JOURNAL PROMPT

Think about your next one-on-one or conversation with a team member, client, peer, or loved one. What's one open-ended question you could ask that would invite more than just facts? Something that opens the door to what they *feel*, *want*, or what's getting in the way.

Now ask yourself: *Am I prepared to hear the honest answer, even if it's unexpected?*

Write that question down. Use it. Then listen without fixing, defending, or redirecting. Just listen.

CHAPTER 8

SPECIFIC FOLLOW-UP QUESTIONS— DIGGING FOR DEPTH

Sometimes, the real story shows up in a throwaway comment.

We were filming a video for a local gym when one of the women we interviewed casually said, "I lost more than a hundred pounds in a year." Then she kept going—on to the next thought, the next question. It almost got left behind. But just before I wrapped the interview, I circled back.

"You mentioned earlier that you lost a hundred pounds in a year. Is that why you started working out?

She paused. Then she told the real story.

"My love for the community here is phenomenal," she said. "It is just as much a physical workout as it is a stress reliever."

It was about finding a safe place. A community. A routine. Emotional healing. Support. Identity. She realized how strong she was and how much stronger she could be through this work. Weight loss? That was just a bonus. And we would've missed all of that if we hadn't asked the follow-up.

Specific follow-up questions are often where the *real* story begins.

WHY WE SKIP THEM

If specific follow-ups are so powerful, why don't we ask them more often?

Here's what gets in the way:

- *We're too focused on our next question.* When we stick to a script, we miss what's happening in real time.

- *We're afraid of going too deep.* What if they get emotional? What if we don't know how to respond?

- *We're multitasking.* Presence is required for follow-ups. If we're distracted or pressed for time, we often miss the invitation to dig deeper.

- *We assume we know.* Our brains crave efficiency, so we fill in gaps instead of pausing to explore them.

But here's the truth: The most powerful question in a conversation is often not the first one, it's the follow-up.

WHY SPECIFIC FOLLOW-UPS MATTER

Follow-up questions signal something powerful: I'm listening. And I care enough to go deeper.

They're the difference between, "Can you say more about that?" and, "When you said you felt invisible, what made you feel that way?"

Neuroscience backs this up. Specific follow-ups:

- Signal engagement
- Activate deeper memory and emotion
- Create a safe space for vulnerability

Here's what's happening under the surface: When someone is asked a specific follow-up, especially one that echoes their own words, it cues the brain to access episodic memory, the system responsible for recalling personal experiences. That's why these moments often come with a pause, a sigh, or a change in tone. The person is not just answering, they're *remembering*.

In that process, parts of the brain like the hippocampus and medial prefrontal cortex light up. These areas are involved in emotional memory, self-awareness, and narrative construction. In plain terms: A good follow-up helps someone make meaning of what they just said.

It's not unusual to hear things like:

- "That's a good question."
- "Wow, I've never been asked that before."
- "Hmm, I haven't thought about it like that."

These aren't just compliments. They're indicators that your question activated something deeper and maybe even something that hadn't been named yet. Let's look at a quick comparison:

Generic Question	Specific Follow-Up
"How did that feel?"	"You mentioned feeling stuck. What did that look like day to day?"
"Can you say more?"	"When you say you lost everything, what comes to mind first?"
"What happened next?"	"What made you finally say yes?"

See the shift? Specific follow-ups loop back to the person's *own words*. They echo. They quote. They reflect. And they often open up something deeper, something that wasn't fully said the first time.

You often see this in:

- Storytelling: the best interviews don't follow a script. They follow the *person*. When something meaningful is said, the interviewer digs in. That's how you get the moment that matters.
- Sales: a client says, "We've tried video before and didn't see results."

A generic response would be: "Oh, sorry to hear that."

A better response would be: "What kind of video was it and what result were you hoping for?"

- Leadership: an employee says, "I'm not sure I'm growing here."

Don't reassure. Ask, "What kind of growth are you hoping for?"

COMMON OPPORTUNITIES TO FOLLOW UP

Everyday conversations are full of quiet invitations to go deeper, but we often let them pass. Here are a few moments where a specific follow-up can shift everything:

- Someone says: "It's been a lot lately."
  Follow-up: "What's been weighing on you the most?"

- They mention: "This reminds me of a hard season."
  Follow-up: "What do you remember most about that time?"

- They say: "I'm fine." (but you sense they're not)
  Follow-up: "What would "better than fine" look like for you right now?"

- They joke to deflect something serious.
  Follow-up: "I noticed you laughed, but I also wondered if there's more to that."

These moments often happen in passing, but when noticed and followed up on, they become windows into real connection.

TRY THIS TECHNIQUE: ECHO AND DRILL

Here's a technique I use all the time:

1. *Echo* a word or phrase they just used.

2. *Drill* into it gently, with care.

For example, they say, "That was the moment everything changed."

You follow with: "Changed how?" or "What made that moment different from the rest?"

That one extra question? That's where the story lives.

JOURNAL PROMPT

Let's make this practical.

1. Take a recent conversation, email, or transcript.

2. Find one phrase that felt important but wasn't explored.

3. Highlight it.

4. Write three specific follow-up questions that dig into it.

5. Ask yourself: Would those questions have revealed more?

Want to go further? Try this live. In your next conversation, listen for an "echo word." Then ask just one more question and watch what opens up.

Anyone can ask a question. It takes presence, attention, and care to ask the second one; the one that makes someone pause and say, "Wow, no one's ever asked me that before."

Specific follow-ups are where the truth lives. They turn curiosity into clarity. They transform a moment into meaning.

So before you move on, practice one follow-up today. Don't rush to the next chapter. Try asking just one more question. And watch what you learn.

CHAPTER 9

CLARIFYING QUESTIONS — THE HINGE BETWEEN CURIOSITY AND CONNECTION

We were halfway through the interview when I realized something wasn't adding up.

Lisa Anderson, the founder and executive director of Room In The Inn-Memphis, was walking me through the organization's mission—how they shelter people experiencing homelessness through a network of churches, offering everything from overnight safety during extreme weather to long-term recovery and housing.

The goal of our project was to create a short documentary that incorporates the work of Room In The Inn-Memphis, but serves as a thought piece in how Memphis is leading the way in homelessness programming and care.

But something she said caught my attention. "This past season we've seen hundreds of children who are living in cars, or on back porches, or in parking lots, abandoned buildings and then coming to us for shelter. So it's been overwhelming this year, the change in the last decade."

I paused and asked a simple clarifying question: "When you say the need is growing, what do you mean? Is the support growing too?"

"We've had a lot of challenges with the number of congregations being so low," she answered.

I clarified: "So, how low are we talking?"

"Right now we only have 32 congregations. That's half what we had before the pandemic."

That's when the picture came into focus: Nearly half of the churches that had volunteered and hosted in 2019 had not returned by 2022. Their need was growing, and people had been turned away more than 1,000 times in the last year. That one clarifying question changed everything.

The purpose of the film shifted. What we thought would be a story about the heart of a long-standing program became a story about loss, compassion, and rebuilding. A call to action. That question didn't just give us a number without context, it gave us the why behind the need. And it gave us the new title of the documentary: *Empty to Enough*.

Clarifying questions are the quiet powerhouses of communication. They don't demand attention, but they command clarity. They simply say, let's slow down and make sure we truly understand what's being said.

In practice, that might sound like:

- "When you say fewer churches are involved, can you give me a sense of how many?"
- "Just to be clear, does that mean participation is down by half?"
- "Can I ask what that looks like day to day?"
- "Help me understand what's changed since the last time this was fully up and running."

These aren't questions that steer the story, they center it. They pull conversations out of assumption and into alignment.

We tend to skip these kinds of questions for one big reason: We think we already know.

Our brains are wired to fill in the gaps. It's efficient, but risky. We may assume alignment when there is none. Or we build strategies, decisions, or stories on half-truths, not because anyone lied, but because we didn't pause long enough to ask.

They also serve another essential function: They create shared understanding. A good clarifying question confirms that both people are seeing the same thing, emphasizing what matters most. It's a way of saying, *"Are we aligned on this?"* or *"Is this the key piece we need to focus on?"* That moment of clarity not only grounds the current conversation—it becomes a reference point for the conversations that follow.

CLARIFYING QUESTIONS AND COGNITIVE BIAS

Two of the biggest culprits in everyday miscommunication are the curse of knowledge and illusory transparency. Clarifying questions help interrupt both.

- *The curse of knowledge* is when we forget what it's like not to know something. We assume what we're saying is obvious, but the person listening may not have the same context, vocabulary, or frame of reference.

- *Illusory transparency* is when we believe our emotions and intentions are more obvious to others than they actually are. We feel like we've made ourselves clear—but often, we haven't.

Clarifying questions work like friction against these biases. They force us to slow down and check what's actually being said and what's actually being heard. They help the speaker realize what they've left unsaid, and help the listener avoid filling in gaps with assumptions.

That's why they're so powerful, especially in leadership, coaching, and collaboration. They don't just clear up confusion, they prevent it in the first place.

Here's a quick example. A few years ago, a nonprofit client hired us to produce a short fundraising video. On one of our early calls, the client said, "We'll need it delivered next month for the gala." The gala was the end of the month, so I nodded and penciled in the mid-month on our project calendar. Seemed obvious.

What they actually meant was that they needed it finished *the beginning* of the month—which was only three weeks away. When I found out, we had to accelerate everything: interviews, scripting, editing, approvals. We made it work, but just barely. It cost us late nights, added stress, and a little bit of the client's confidence in our process. It's not just the big misunderstandings that cost us. It's the little ones. Clarification protects the relationship and the result.

All of that could've been prevented with one simple clarifying question: "Just to confirm, what's the exact date you're targeting for delivery?"

That's why these questions are so powerful—especially in leadership, coaching, and collaboration. They don't just clear up confusion. They prevent it from happening in the first place. Clarification protects the relationship and the result.

Let's be clear: Clarifying questions aren't about poking holes. They're about pulling focus. You're not doubting the speaker. You're honoring the conversation by checking that you truly understand. Asking for clarity doesn't make you look uninformed—it makes you someone worth trusting.

HOW TO CLARIFY WITHOUT SOUNDING CONFRONTATIONAL

Here's the key: It's not just what you ask, it's how you ask it.

Clarifying questions should come from a place of curiosity, not correction. The goal isn't to catch someone in a contradiction.

It's to better understand their reality. That's what makes people feel safe and seen.

A few go-to phrases I return to often:

- "Just to make sure I'm following you …"
- "Can I check my understanding real quick?"
- "When you said ____, did you mean ____?"
- "Help me see the picture you're seeing."

Tone matters. Curiosity softens what could otherwise feel like confrontation. And when we're truly open to hearing the answer—even if it's different than we expected—the other person can feel that.

THE PSYCHOLOGY OF CLARIFICATION

Clarifying questions do more than correct the record, they calm the brain.

When people feel misunderstood, even slightly, it activates the brain's threat response—a survival mechanism designed to protect us. This response originates in the amygdala, the part of the brain that scans for danger. When something feels off—a miscommunication, a confusing comment, an ambiguous tone—the brain treats it like a potential threat. It triggers a stress response: heart rate increases, defenses go up, and we stop listening and start reacting.

Everyone has felt it: that flash of irritation when someone gets their words wrong. That subtle tension when they sense they're not being heard. The conversation gets tighter, faster, less productive.

But when someone pauses and says, "Can I make sure I heard you right?" or "Just to clarify ..." it signals care, not correction.

It tells the brain: *You're safe. You're seen. You're heard.*

That moment of clarity becomes a moment of trust.

Clarifying also slows the conversation just enough to allow for reflection. That benefits both people:

- The speaker gets to go deeper or reframe.
- The listener resists the urge to jump to conclusions.

The result? A more grounded conversation where both sides feel understood. You'll find clarifying questions everywhere once you start looking:

- In a one-on-one: "You mentioned feeling a bit stressed, and now you've said you're spending long hours on this project—are those connected?"

- In crisis communication: "What do we know right now?" becomes a grounding question that cuts through chaos and aligns the team.

- In creative projects: "When you say 'clean and modern,' do you have an example in mind?" helps define a shared vision before time is wasted.

- In negotiation: "You said timeline is important. What would 'on time' look like for you?" clarifies expectations before assumptions take root.

- In team culture: When teams normalize clarifying questions, they reduce rework, resentment, and resignation—and replace it with alignment, clarity, and trust.

When used with intention, clarifying questions prevent confusion and build confidence, connection, and momentum.

Think about a recent conversation where you thought you understood, but later realized you didn't. What might have shifted if you had asked one simple, clarifying question?

Now think ahead. What conversation is on your calendar this week where you could practice slowing down to clarify and connect?

Challenge yourself to ask at least one clarifying question at that moment. Something as simple as:

"Can I make sure I'm getting this right?"

"What does that look like for you?"

"What do you mean when you say ___?"

Then pause. Listen. Let the clarity guide the next question.

Think of a time you've said, "That's not what I meant," or a time someone said it to you.

Write a short summary of the miscommunication.

Now, imagine you could rewind. What clarifying question might have prevented the misunderstanding?

Write one to two alternate questions you might use next time. Keep this list somewhere visible this week. It'll sharpen your conversations and your leadership.

And once you've clarified what's being said, the next step is often the hardest and most powerful: *listen fully.*

CHAPTER 10

ACTIVE LISTENING — THE QUIET SKILL THAT CHANGES EVERYTHING

Sometimes, what people don't say tells you everything.

In documentary interviews, this happens all the time: a small pause, a shift in tone, a glance off-camera. The real story lives beneath the polished answers, underneath the practiced lines; but you'll only catch it if you're truly listening.

Carl Rogers, one of the most influential psychologists of the twentieth century, believed that deep, nonjudgmental listening was the foundation of connection and change. He called it unconditional positive regard.[12]

To Rogers, active listening wasn't about waiting for your turn to speak. It was about listening to understand, not to respond or fix. Just to be fully present with another human being. This practice became a cornerstone in psychology, but its power extends far beyond therapy.

- In leadership, it builds trust.
- In storytelling, it reveals truth.
- In everyday life, it reminds people they matter.

When someone feels truly heard, especially in moments of uncertainty or vulnerability, their brain shifts out of defense mode. The nervous system relaxes. The prefrontal cortex lights up. They start to open up.

Neuroscience backs this up. Genuine listening lowers cortisol (stress), increases oxytocin (connection), and creates interpersonal synchrony when two people's brains begin to mirror each other in rhythm and response. In other words, people lean in when you lean in.[12]

PRESENCE OVER PERFORMANCE

I'm a busy person, and I don't say that as a badge of honor. I say it as the reality of being a business owner, a leader, a do-er, and someone who generally thrives when juggling a lot at once.

But what I've learned (sometimes the hard way) is that my busyness can create distance. It can make others feel like I'm "fitting them in" instead of truly showing up. I've caught myself glancing at the clock, trying to stay on schedule (I'm notoriously optimistic with time), only to realize later I wasn't really there.

To be clear, I'm not proud of that. I've started practicing small shifts that help me stay grounded and present, especially in one-on-one conversations. Here's what I've been doing:

- Putting my phone away or screen-side-down
- Keeping eye contact
- Paraphrasing what they said before responding
- Asking follow-ups instead of offering quick fixes
- Letting go of the clock when the moment calls for it

And I'm noticing it's making a big difference. Recently, however, in a one-on-one with a team member, they made an offhand comment: "I know you won't be around for a while ..."

They moved past it so quickly, I almost let it go. But at the end of the meeting, I paused and circled back. I asked a clarifying question (see what I did there?) and invited them to say more.

They told me that when I travel a lot or have back-to-back projects, they don't see me as much and they miss these conversations. That was their way of saying, I need to feel seen. I need to feel heard.

It hit me. Active listening doesn't require hours, it requires presence. Presence can be as simple as putting down your phone and looking someone in the eye when they speak.

NOT ALL LISTENING IS EQUAL

There's a big difference between:

- **Passive listening**: You hear words, but you're not really engaged (think: nodding on Zoom while reading emails).

- **Selective listening**: You're tuning in only when something seems relevant to *you*.

- **Active listening**: You're fully present tuned into words, tone, body language, and emotion.

Great leaders and interviewers listen with their whole selves. They watch posture. They notice pacing. They hear the sigh after the sentence. They don't fill the silence. They *sit* in it.

That's when the truth comes out.

Techniques to Practice Active Listening	
Mirror & Paraphrase	Repeat back what you heard, not word for word, but in essence. "What I'm hearing is that you felt both relieved and uncertain at the same time?"
Wait Three Seconds	After someone finishes speaking, pause. Don't jump in. Let the silence do its job.
Name the Emotion	"You sound frustrated. Am I getting that right?" Just naming it can help someone feel seen.
Watch the Nonverbal	People might say "I'm fine" with words but their tone, posture, or eyes may tell a different story.
Remove Your Agenda	This is the hardest part. Let go of the outcome you want and be curious about their truth.

Think of someone in your life—a teammate, friend, or partner—you'd like to better understand. Set aside 10 minutes for a conversation where your only goal is to listen.

Start with a simple open-ended question like:

- *What's something you're proud of right now?*
- *What's been on your mind lately?*

As they speak, focus solely on understanding, not responding. Try reflecting back what you hear:

- *"What I'm hearing is … "*
- *"It sounds like … "*
- *"I noticed your tone shifted when you said that. What's that about?"*

Afterward, journal about the experience:

- How did it feel to listen without offering advice or opinions?
- What surprised you?
- What shifted in your understanding or connection?
- How might this kind of listening change your conversations at work—or at home?

Remember: Active listening is quiet work. You may not get credit for it, but it's often the difference between being heard and being trusted.

CHAPTER 11

REFLECTION QUESTIONS — DISCOVERING INSIGHT AND SELF-AWARENESS

Reflection questions are often quiet, but they're rarely small. Whether they're asked in a journal, a one-on-one meeting, or a team debrief, they have the power to turn experience into insight—and insight into action. This chapter explores how reflection questions fuel personal growth *and* collective learning, helping leaders pause, process, and move forward with greater clarity.

I was sitting in John's office, the low hum of a lawnmower outside, and a notebook on the table next to me. John was my business coach. We met once a month to talk through the challenges, the wins, and the stuck spots in my business. And if there was one thing he'd do consistently, it was ask questions that didn't just make me think, they made me change.

That day, I was venting.

We were busy on paper, that should have felt good. But the truth? The work was underfunded. Several projects had been discounted. A few were sponsorships for longtime nonprofit clients we believed in. I told John we were helping people, being generous, making it work. I said it like I was defending a noble decision.

He looked at me thoughtfully and asked, "Are you being generous, or altruistic?"

I paused. I blinked. Was there a difference? I hadn't considered them in contrast to each other. So I didn't have an answer for him in the moment.

After our session, I got back to the office, still perplexed, and looked it up. Generosity is giving more than expected. Altruism is giving to the point of self-sacrifice.

That question hit hard. Not because it was accusatory, but because it exposed something I hadn't named. What I thought was generosity was actually something else: a pattern of giving that was coming at the expense of my time, my energy, and the sustainability of my business.

That single question helped me see a belief I'd been carrying for a long time: Service as a business core value meant service must happen even when it costs me. Was that true? Even if it wrecked my team? That belief had gone unrecognized, and because of that, it had shaped more decisions than I realized about my calendar, my client boundaries, even how I showed up for my family.

The answer didn't always change my decisions, but it gave me clarity about my motivation, and with clarity comes choice.

That's the power of a reflection question. It doesn't push. It doesn't pressure.

It gently invites you to look inward, to shift from doing into noticing. To name something you've been living, but not yet questioning.

While that question from my coach sparked a personal shift, I've also seen how reflection questions can do the same for teams. When used well, they help organizations make sense of challenges, celebrate what's working, and identify where to go next. The process may look different, but the purpose is the same: to uncover meaning that drives momentum.

While open-ended, clarifying, and follow-up questions help you explore *outward*, reflection questions help you look *inward*.

They prompt: pause, perspective, and personal truth.

They're the kind of questions great coaches, mentors, and leaders ask, not when they're trying to solve a problem, but when they're helping you uncover what's beneath it. And they don't have to be dramatic to be powerful. They can sound like:

- "What's driving that choice?"
- "What does this really mean to you?"

- "What are you learning about yourself through this?"
- "What would you do differently next time?"

WHY REFLECTION QUESTIONS WORK

Neuroscience tells us that introspection activates the default mode network, a part of the brain that lights up when we're thinking about our own thoughts. It's the internal workspace of imagination, memory, empathy, and insight.[12]

Reflection questions activate this space. They create integration, where emotional experience meets conscious insight. This is where creativity blooms, values align, and leadership ideals deepen. Leaders who build reflection into their routines don't just grow faster, they grow *wiser*.[13]

REFLECTION IN DIFFERENT AREAS

In coaching, reflection questions are key. They don't fix, they facilitate. They help people surface what they already know but haven't yet named.

In leadership, they bring clarity to complex moments:

- "What decision would you make if fear weren't in the way?"
- "What outcome would you be proud of one year from now?"

In organizations, reflection fuels innovation. Retrospectives, after-action reviews, and post-mortems often center around core questions:

- What made us successful?
- What caused missteps or near-misses?
- What did we encounter that we didn't anticipate?
- What should we try next time?

Reflection is what turns experience into growth.

If you run a business of any kind, you've probably revamped your sales process a few dozen times. I know I have.

During one of those iterations, I added a new question to our discovery calls: "What's your biggest roadblock?"

The responses stopped people in their tracks.

- "No one has ever asked me that."
- "Sigh ... that's a really good question."
- "Hmmm, come to think of it ..."
- "Wow. I've never thought about this before."

It was like watching people shift from autopilot to awareness.

Sometimes they answered quickly. Other times, they paused. Reflected. Let the answer surface in silence.

That one question created both connection and momentum. It revealed pain points and gave clarity they didn't have before.

Reflection questions don't just belong in coaching or journaling. They can impact a sale, grow a business, or change a habit.

How to Use Reflection Questions Well	
Guideline	Description
Ask Without Judgment	Tone matters. Reflection questions only work when people feel safe to answer honestly.
Make Room for Silence	These aren't rapid-fire. Ask and wait. Let the pause do the work.
Use Reflection to Summarize	You can mirror the conversation back: "It sounds like you've been doing a lot of giving lately. How is that affecting you?
Reflect with Yourself, too	These tools aren't just for others. They're also for you. Leaders who reflect, lead better.

JOURNAL PROMPT

Take a few minutes to journal your response to these:

- What have I been giving my energy to, and is it aligned with what matters most?

- Where in my life am I feeling stretched thin, and why?

- What am I learning about myself right now?

- What decision would I make if I trusted myself more?

- What's one thing I can stop doing that would make space for what I need?

No need to overthink. Just write what comes.

These questions aren't about getting it "right." They're about getting *real*.

Reflection questions don't demand immediate answers. They don't rush clarity. They linger. They expand. They help people grow into the answers over time.

When paired with the other tools in the Question Lens™ and OSCARS framework, reflection questions become a gentle nudge toward deeper understanding. Not just of others, but mostly for ourselves.

CHAPTER 12

SHARE A LITTLE OF YOURSELF —
BUILDING TRUST THROUGH RECIPROCITY

Sometimes, even when you ask the best questions, the person on the other side just doesn't open up.

You listen. You clarify. You ask follow-ups. You reflect. But their answers stay short, surface-level, and guarded. I've been there, especially in leadership conversations.

One-on-one meetings are a regular rhythm in my company, and I take them seriously. I prepare. I ask curious questions. I genuinely want to know what's going on beneath the surface. But not everyone's ready or willing to go there.

There was one team member early on in my company who stood out. Let's call her Caitlin.

In every one-on-one, I tried to meet Caitlin with openness. I asked about her work, her goals, her stressors. I even shared a little about my own journey, mistakes I'd made, lessons I'd learned. I hoped that vulnerability might create space for hers.

But week after week, I'd get short, clipped answers. One-sentence updates. Polite deflections. Shrugs. They were the shortest one-on-ones on record. No matter the approach, the answers seemed to be the same.

I began to believe she didn't trust me. What about my leadership made her feel unsafe to share? It seemed clear that she didn't trust me with the truth. Not wanting to take it personally, I continued to observe as the months went by. In several instances, it seemed she may not trust herself to speak the truth out loud. It was just unfamiliar territory. Ultimately, you can't force connection, but you *can* model it.

Sometimes, sharing a little bit of yourself is the invitation someone needs, even if they don't take it right away. Unlike the instance in Chapter 7, it doesn't always turn out positive in the end. I never found a way in with Caitlin. Despite keeping the regular check-ins, frustrating as they often felt, she decided to exit the company on her own. She was a solid performer individually but never really connected with me or with the team. Friendly, but not connected. In this instance, I don't think she ever truly opened up. All I could do was model through my own sharing and vulnerability. And that's sometimes all you can do too.

People are complex and we never know what they're walking in the door with. Sharing a little of yourself does work though.

How often do we bump into someone and they ask, "How are you?" Most of us default to, "Good!" or "Busy," and the conversation ends there.

But what if you gave just a little more?

At client events or fundraisers, I often challenge my team to rethink their response to the usual "How's business?"—to share something real and specific.

Instead of saying, "Busy, but good," they might say, "It's going well! We just wrapped a project about street design and how it translates into safer neighborhoods. It was really inspiring. What about you—been inspired by anything lately?"

It's not a long story. It's a quick window into something meaningful—and it shifts the conversation. More often than not, the other person responds with something thoughtful too. That little bit of sharing? It gives them permission to do the same.

WHY SHARING WORKS

Psychologists call it the norm of reciprocity: a social principle that suggests when someone does something for us, we naturally feel inclined to return the gesture. When someone opens up, we're more likely to open up in return.[14]

In conversations, this looks like:

- A leader sharing a moment of self-doubt to invite real talk from a team member
- A coach revealing a personal insight to build trust
- A journalist offering a glimpse of themselves to make an interviewee more comfortable

Sharing builds bridges, not by shifting focus, but by signaling: "This is a safe space. I'm not above you. I'm right here with you."

I found a unique way to build that bridge. In April 2022, I was on vacation with my family in Newport Beach, California, when I finally decided to get my second tattoo.

For months, I'd been trying out temporary tattoos—little crescent moons, full moons, lunar phases—placing them on different parts of my arm. Testing. Waiting. Wondering if I'd regret it.

But the moon has always meant something to my family and me. A full moon means Grandpa and Grandma are watching over us. A new moon means the sky is dark enough to see the stars. An eclipse reminds us that even the unexpected can be awe-inspiring. The phases show us that everything changes— and that's the point.

I was drawn to the moon's quiet presence and the way it shifts as the calendar shifts (or, more accurately, as the Earth moves). So I had the phases of the moon tattooed on my forearm.

To me, it's a reminder of two things:

- You can always reflect the light, even if it's just a sliver.
- Everything happens in phases. Life will change, and so will you.

Eventually I realized it's also a metaphor for connection and leadership.

Just like the moon, people don't always show their full selves. Sometimes, in a conversation or team meeting, what you get is a sliver—a hint of what's going on beneath the surface. Other times, someone opens up fully and floods the space with light.

And like the moon, it's not about forcing the change. There's patience required. It's about presence. Timing. Trust.

That tattoo? It's become one of my favorite tools in building trust.

When I meet someone new, especially in interviews or leadership settings, if I notice a tattoo, I often share that I have one too and ask about theirs.

What happens next is almost always the same: they open up. They tell a story. They offer something real.

And I didn't have to ask a deep question or press for vulnerability. I just shared a little of myself. A quiet cue: *It's safe here. I'm human too.*

WHEN TO SHARE AND WHEN NOT TO

Sharing isn't about making the conversation about *you*. It's about creating the conditions for others to be real.

Do share when:

- You sense the other person needs permission to go deeper
- You want to normalize vulnerability
- You're building trust in a new relationship

Don't share when:

- You're shifting the spotlight to avoid discomfort
- You're dominating the conversation with your story
- The moment calls for listening, not relating

The goal is to open the door, not to walk through it and start redecorating. You don't have to launch into your life story to build trust. Here are a few ways to open the door:

- "I've struggled with that too."
- "I remember going through something similar. It felt really heavy at the time."
- "I'm working on that myself. You're not alone."
- "I've had to learn that lesson the hard way. I'm still learning, honestly."

Short. Honest. Grounded in humility. Then gently shift the spotlight back with a reflective question.

Sometimes, you'll share and still get silence. That's okay. Trust isn't always built in one conversation, and vulnerability isn't always immediate. Think of it like planting a seed, not delivering a script. You can model openness and give people a taste of what's possible, but you can't control when or if they decide to reciprocate. Safety varies, especially in work and business conversations. Try not to feel limited by that boundary. We bring ourselves to work and business, an appropriate personal share does wonderful things.

Sometimes, they're just not ready. And that's not failure, it's an invitation to keep modeling, in hopes that they eventually open up too.

JOURNAL PROMPT

Think of a recent conversation where the other person held back. Now ask yourself:

- Did I share anything real about myself?
- Did I create enough space and safety for vulnerability?
- Did I model the kind of conversation I was hoping to have?

Now craft a short response to a common question like, "How are you?" or "How's work going?" where you share something real but still keep the focus on the other person.

Example: "Honestly? It's been a heavy week, some wins and some hard stuff. But I'd love to hear how *you're* doing."

Small disclosures. Big ripples.

CLOSING THE LOOP

MASTERING THE QUESTION LENS™

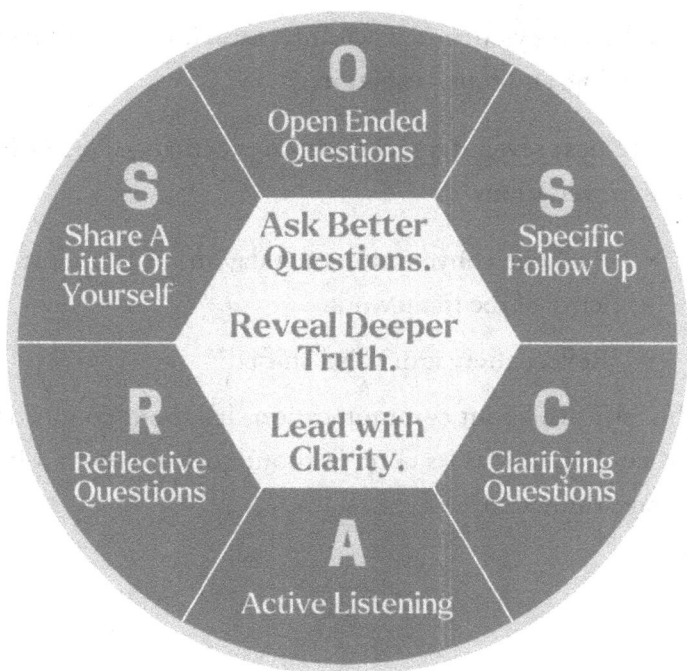

By now, you've explored each piece of OSCARS in the Question Lens™ method:

- **Open-Ended Questions** that invite details
- **Specific Follow-Up Questions** that dig deeper
- **Clarifying Questions** that prevent assumption
- **Active Listening** that creates presence
- **Reflection Questions** that invite insight
- **Sharing a Little of Yourself** to build trust and reciprocity

Together, they form a cycle of connection, leadership, storytelling, and transformation.

For the next seven days, commit to practicing OSCARS in daily conversations.

- Pick one conversation each day to focus on just one letter of the framework.
- Reflect afterward: What shifted?

This isn't just about communication. It's about connection, and connection, at its core, is about curiosity with a little courage thrown in.

PART 3

QUESTIONS IN ACTION: LIVING AND LEADING WITH CURIOSITY

CHAPTER 13

THE QUESTION-DRIVEN LEADER — STORIES FROM MY LEADERSHIP JOURNEY

Leadership isn't about having all the answers, it's about having the courage to ask the right questions. Questions that inspire, engage, challenge, and sometimes unravel you. The hardest questions, the ones that change us, are rarely the ones we ask of others, they're the ones we learn to ask ourselves. In the previous chapters I've referred to these as reflective questions. But in this chapter, we're talking about going inward, deep in your mind and your thoughts to uncover your own truth in the answers.

I learned this the hard way, just a few years into leading a team at my company. At the time, it was one of my lowest leadership moments. If only I had known what I know now.

A LEADERSHIP CRISIS AND THE QUESTION THAT CHANGED EVERYTHING

We were on the edge of something big, both personally and professionally. One of our team members called a meeting to let us know they were leaving for personal reasons. It was heartfelt and thoughtful. We had time to plan, and we knew it would be best. I was also in logistics mode, thinking about how I would replace them and what it would look like to continue operating at our growing pace in their absence.

The next day, my husband and I signed the paperwork to buy our first commercial building. Our company was expanding. We'd have a studio, more space, and for the first time in my career, I'd have my own office. It was thrilling and terrifying all at once.

What came the following day completely blindsided me. Another employee, a key one, told us they were leaving to work for a competitor. Unlike the first, this one was sharp, personal, and gutwrenching. While it was never communicated directly, it seemed clear they were leaving, in part, because of me: my leadership, my presence, my approach.

I didn't handle it well. My first reaction was anger. In fact, I essentially stomped out of the office—not literally, but I did leave early that day, and it was clear I was angry.

That night, I crumbled on the couch. I went through every conversation with my husband, who was still working in a corporate job at the time (while serving as our part-time bookkeeper, human resources, and IT guy). I thought about quitting. I even considered walking away from the building we'd just signed for. Selling it all. Starting over or stopping altogether.

The next few days were harder. I overheard a whispered conversation. It was one that I wish I had never heard. It stayed with me:

- "She gets in the way all the time."
- "She shares too much in the office."
- "All she cares about is money and posting on social media."
- "The company wouldn't go anywhere if it weren't for her husband."

Those words were painful to hear, and even worse, I wasn't meant to hear them. How could I possibly address them if they weren't said to me?

I was so dejected and angry and wanted to respond. There were reasons for all of it. This employee was young. There were lots of things they didn't know and obstacles I silently cleared, especially sales, so they could focus on creative work. Business was slow and I was working so hard to keep the team employed. It made me angry that I knew I was doing so much to help them grow and be successful only to be met with frustration and anger. As I tried to process what to do next, a wise mentor asked me the question that would change everything: "There's a little bit of truth in statements made in anger. What about their angry statements could be true? And what about them is not true?"

As a leader, I had to face that head-on. I had plenty of reasons to write off what they said. But growth comes from hard things. It forced me to face something difficult.

Over the next few months, I reflected and recalibrated. I realized:

- I *was* getting in the way of the creative process.
- I *had* crossed unspoken boundaries.
- I *was* focused on growth. So much so that it looked like I only cared about money.

But I also reminded myself what was *not* true:

- I deeply believed in the power of our work.
- I cared deeply about our team.
- I had sacrificed a lot to keep jobs secure.
- As my husband told me, "tracking the money doesn't make a business." I *was* running the company and leading it to be successful.

So, I started asking better questions:

- What would it take to rebuild trust, even if only in new hires?
- How could I empower the team around me, not only as they start, but also as they grew?
- What kind of leadership did this company really need?

- How could I bring the team along with appropriate realities of small business?

- How could I grow without losing myself or my team?

HOW I WISH I HAD USED THE QUESTION LENS™ SOONER

Looking back, one of my biggest regrets isn't that people left, it's that I didn't ask better questions before they did.

If I had applied the OSCARS framework, especially in the months prior to their exits, I might have opened doors to honest dialogue, rather than closed chapters. Imagine if I had:

- **Asked Open-Ended Questions** like:
  "What do you need right now to grow here?"
  "What do you wish this role offered that it currently doesn't?"

- **Followed Up Specifically** when someone mentioned "burnout" or "feeling stuck""
  "When you say burnout, what's causing it most? Is it the workload, the type of work, or something else?"

- **Clarified Assumptions** about my leadership:
  "Can you share more about what made you feel unsupported?"
  "What moments stand out that changed how you saw me as a leader?"

- **Listened Actively**, not to respond or fix, but to truly understand. Noticing what wasn't said. Pausing to reflect instead of defend.

- **Reflected Back** their words:
  "You said you felt like your ideas didn't matter. Has that been a growing feeling, or is it tied to something specific?"

- **Shared a Little of Myself**, not to center the conversation on me, but to create space for them:
  "I remember a time when I felt like I outgrew a role too. It's hard to admit, even to ourselves. And even as your leader."

Maybe some of them still would have left, and that's okay. People grow. Chapters close. But what clarity might we all have received if I wasn't afraid to ask?

Maybe I would have better understood what they needed. Maybe I could have helped them step into something new, within or beyond our company, with clarity and support. Maybe they would've left feeling heard, not hurt. And I would've led with curiosity instead of control.

That's what a question-driven leader does.

THE SHIFT: FROM REACTION TO REDESIGN

The questions I asked led to three major shifts:

1. **My husband joined the company full-time** as Director of Operations. He built policies and hiring systems that respected boundaries, set clear expectations, and enabled sustainable growth. It also took some things off my plate. This gave the team an

alternative to me in leadership. If they weren't sure how to tell me something, they could share it with him.

2. **I stepped into a visionary role**, focusing on big-picture strategy and building a team capable of executing the details with excellence. I actively tried to hand-off specific tasks and remove myself as an obstacle.

3. **We completed the office build-out.** This gave me an office, not for status, but to have a place for conversations that didn't need to be had with everyone in the room. There was also a phone-call room to give them the same opportunity.

It took a long time and a lot of reflection. And I was forever changed. I eventually let go of the hurt. I remembered that the harshest words often come from people who don't know the full story. I decided that I had many areas to improve and rather than be angry, I needed to directly address what they said that was true, even if they would never see it. I chose curiosity over bitterness. I chose growth.

Leadership is full of messy, unscripted, deeply human moments. We don't get to control all the outcomes. But we do get to decide what questions we'll ask of others, and of ourselves. That decision shapes everything.

In the next chapter, we'll widen the lens and explore how questioning our belief systems, assumptions, identities, and the invisible rules we live by, can lead to sharper decision-making and more courageous leadership.

The questions that shaped my leadership weren't always mine—they came from mentors, team members, and even difficult situations. The real shift happened when I learned to turn those same kinds of questions inward. As you reflect on your own journey, use these prompts to uncover the questions that will help you grow.

1. Recall a pivotal moment in your leadership.

    What was the hardest question you asked yourself, and how did it change your next step?

2. Think of a time you received feedback that was hard to hear.

    What part was true? What wasn't? How does separating the two shift your perspective?

3. Identify a leadership challenge you're facing now.

    What open-ended or clarifying questions could help you see it more clearly?

4. Reflect on a moment when you reacted instead of reflecting.

    How might that moment have unfolded differently if you had paused to ask a better question?

CHAPTER 14

PHILOSOPHY IN PRACTICE — HOW QUESTIONING YOUR BELIEF SYSTEMS CAN SHARPEN LEADERSHIP

We tend to think our beliefs are facts. But more often, they're just stories we've repeated so many times we stop questioning them. In leadership and in life, those unexamined beliefs can quietly shape every decision we make. Until one day, a question disrupts them.

THE BELIEF THAT HELD ME BACK

In the last chapter, I shared the story of a painful leadership moment that made me question everything. But I didn't learn what was happening beneath the surface until later. Because beneath every hard conversation, every misstep, every resignation, there was a deeper belief driving my decisions: *I wanted to be liked.*

Because I wanted to be liked, I wasn't leading with clarity or conviction. I was leading like a host planning a fun night out, making sure everyone was having a good time, avoiding conflict, keeping the vibes high. Not because I didn't care, but because I cared so much about being seen as kind, generous, and fun, that I was afraid to disappoint anyone. And I most certainly didn't want to be like any "bad boss" I ever had in my career.

That belief that "being liked is more important than being right" was holding me back. It was clouding my ability to make the kinds of decisions real leadership requires. I needed clarity, boundaries, and vision.

People don't just want a fun boss, they want direction. They want to know what success looks like. They want to trust that when things get hard, their leader won't disappear into people-pleasing. They want to feel secure, not coddled.

I wasn't doing that at all. I was clearing obstacles, trying to only assign "fun" projects, and giving feedback that was always positive. I was not helping them grow through challenges, diversify their skills, nor was I giving clear and constructive feedback.

What helped me name that belief, and begin to rewrite it, wasn't just a coach or a therapist (though they were both instrumental). It was a decision to stop coasting on instinct and start digging deeper into what I actually believed. That journey led me to something I never expected to be drawn to: philosophy. Specifically, the Stoics.

STOICISM AS A TOOL FOR LEADERSHIP

I didn't start reading Marcus Aurelius or Epictetus because I wanted to become a philosopher. I started because I wanted to become a better leader, a more grounded human, and someone who could handle hard things without falling apart or letting their emotions write the narrative.

Stoicism is an ancient philosophy rooted in clarity, reason, and acceptance. At its core, it teaches that:

- **Virtue is the highest good.** Qualities like courage, wisdom, and justice matter more than status or success. Doing the right thing because it's the right thing.

- **Control is limited.** We control our choices, not the outcomes.

- **Adversity is a teacher.** Hardship isn't something to avoid, it's something to learn from.

That third point changed me. When I looked at my leadership breakdown through a Stoic lens, I stopped seeing it as a failure and started seeing it as a teacher.

I asked myself, *What if this isn't a setback? What if this is the invitation?*

That shift in thinking sharpened my decision-making. It made me less reactive, more reflective. Less focused on proving myself, more focused on improving myself. It helped me see that my old beliefs weren't "bad," they were just outdated. They were formed by younger versions of me who needed approval to feel safe. A version of me who was growing myself and my confidence. Versions who hadn't yet led a team or built a business or made payroll during a pandemic.

I'm not that version anymore, and neither are you.

You don't need to become a Stoic to benefit from philosophy. You just need to become someone who's willing to pause and ask:

- Why do I believe this?
- Where did this assumption come from?
- Is this still serving me, or is it just familiar?

I've made better decisions ever since I started asking those questions.

For example: I used to avoid giving direct feedback because I thought it would make people feel bad and they'd resent me. But when I challenged that belief and started asking, "What do they need in order to grow?" I realized that avoiding feedback wasn't kindness, it was fear. So I changed my approach. I got clearer. Kinder. Braver.

The result was that my team didn't crumble, they grew. It wasn't instantaneous. I had to build a rhythm of feedback. They had to know I cared about growth and was on their team. They had to know I was willing to listen. They had to know I was growing too.

If you want to engage philosophy to advance your leadership, you don't need a textbook. You just need a few good questions:

- What belief might be shaping my decisions right now?
- Where did that belief come from and is it still true for me?
- What new belief would serve me better?
- What fear is underneath the belief I'm holding onto?

These questions won't always give you immediate answers, but they'll give you something better: perspective. And perspective leads to power. When you treat belief as a living framework, something to be revisited, re-evaluated, reshaped, you step into a new kind of leadership. One rooted in awareness, not assumption. One fueled by questions, not ego.

That's the gift of philosophy in practice. Not certainty, but wisdom. And it starts with a question.

CHAPTER 15

WHEN QUESTIONS AREN'T CURIOUS

You believe in the power of a question. So do I. But I've learned that not all questions are created equal. Some illuminate, while others—often unintentionally—shame, shut down, or signal judgment.

When I first started telling people I was writing a book, most were supportive, but some asked questions like:

- "Why would you write a book?"
- "Who's going to read it?"
- "That sounds expensive. How much does it cost?"
- "What if no one reads it?"

They weren't asking to understand. In the best case, they were asking to protect, but they were projecting their own fears or assumptions. Those questions didn't feel curious to me, they felt like subtle attacks. The tone and phrasing is important. The same words, said differently, hit differently.

This chapter is about the kinds of questions we should ask sparingly, if at all. Here are five question traps that cause more harm than good:

1. Leading Questions

These questions *sound* like inquiry but are actually statements in disguise. They funnel the person toward the answer you already believe is true.

- "Don't you think this might be a little too ambitious?"
- "Wouldn't it be smarter to wait until you're more established?"
- "Haven't we tried this before?"

Why it's harmful: It erodes trust. You're guiding, not listening.

Instead ask: "What's making this the right time for you to take this leap?"

2. Projecting Questions

These come from *your* experience, but are posed as concern for someone else.

- "Are you sure this won't burn you out? I tried something like that and regretted it."
- "How are you going to manage that on top of everything else?"

Why it's harmful: You're projecting your story onto theirs. It assumes sameness and can feel like doubt dressed as advice.

Instead ask: "What support systems are you building around this?"

3. Accusatory Questions

They assume wrongdoing, often passive-aggressively, and rarely leave room for clarity or nuance.

- "Why didn't you tell me about this sooner?"
- "How long have you known this?"
- "What were you thinking?"

Why it's harmful: These questions shut people down, create shame, and sabotage psychological safety.

Instead ask: "Can you help me understand your thought process?"

4. True/False Questions

Some questions force binary thinking when the truth lives in the grey.

- "So is this a success or a failure?"
- "Are you happy with how that turned out? Or do you regret it?"

Why it's harmful: It ignores complexity. It flattens nuance.

Instead ask: "What parts of this feel aligned? What parts don't?"

5. Yes/No Questions

Not all yes/no questions are bad—"Do you want coffee?" is perfectly fine. But when used for emotionally layered topics, they can shut down real dialogue.

- "Are you happy here?"
- "Do you believe in this project?"

Why it's harmful: It rushes to conclusions. It bypasses context.

Instead ask: "What's your experience been like here so far?"

It's not just the question, it's the *intention* behind it. It's the *tone* that wraps it. It's whether you're asking to connect or to control.

A BETTER WAY FORWARD

The Question Lens™ exists to help us ask better questions, but it also teaches us that asking is not neutral, it's powerful. And power comes with responsibility.

So next time you find yourself about to ask someone a question, pause and ask:

- Am I leading or listening?
- Am I projecting or perceiving?
- Am I curious or controlling?

Questions can open hearts or close them. Make sure yours do the former.

WHEN I GOT IT WRONG

One time I sat down one-on-one with a team member who had dropped the ball on a big project. I had reviewed everything. I knew, deep down, it came down to poor preparation. So I opened our conversation with this question: "Were you prepared and focused ahead of this project?"

Before I even finished the sentence, I saw it happen. Their posture stiffened. Their tone changed. They got defensive—and so did I. The rest of the conversation was unproductive. We both walked away frustrated and unresolved.

Why? Because I led with a question that accused, not one that invited reflection. I started with blame instead of curiosity.

If I could go back, here's how I'd reframe that moment:

- "Walk me through how you prepared for this project."
- "Can you give me a step-by-step of what you did?"
- "Was there anything missing from the process?"
- "How was this different from the last project?"
- "What can we do together to prevent this in the future?"

That's not interrogation, that's dialogue. And more importantly, it signals something vital: I believe there's more to this story and I'm curious to understand it with you.

PAUSE BEFORE YOU ASK

So here's the invitation: before your next question leaves your lips, pause. Ask yourself:

- Am I asking to understand or to assert?
- Am I speaking from curiosity or from fear?
- Will this question open the conversation or shut it down?
- Could I be projecting something that isn't theirs to carry?
- What's my intention, and how might it land?

When we ask questions with intention, we create space for clarity, safety, and truth.

The goal isn't just to ask more questions. The goal is to ask better ones, the kind that reveal truth, not bury it.

Take a moment to reflect on your own question asking habits, not just what you ask, but how and why you ask.

1. **Think back to a time you asked a question that didn't land well.**

   o   What was your intention at that moment?

   o   How might the tone or wording have felt to the other person?

2. **Consider a recent time someone asked *you* a question that felt judgmental or fear-based.**

   o   What made it feel that way?

   o   How did you respond externally and internally?

3. **Choose one relationship or team dynamic where you want to build more trust.**

   o   What kinds of questions can you ask to create openness instead of defensiveness?

   o   Try replacing one yes/no or accusatory question with a curious, open-ended alternative this week.

CHAPTER 16

MAKE IT A HABIT

Curiosity is not a personality trait, it's a practice, a discipline, a habit.

It sounds counterintuitive, doesn't it? Especially coming from someone like me who has built a career on curiosity. You'd think that asking questions would come easily. And it does, to an extent. But natural curiosity comes naturally or not, intentional inquiry is possible for everyone. And it applies every bit to questions of ourselves as it does to questions of others.

THE LUNCH THAT SPARKED A SHIFT

"Lauren, do you ever make time to just think?" a friend asked me over lunch.

I laughed. "Sure, I think a lot! What do you mean?"

"Well, I mean, do you *schedule* time to think? About what you want, where you're going, what success looks like for your business and your life?"

That's when it hit me. I didn't make time to think. Not like that and not on purpose. I certainly didn't make time to *ask myself* questions. Maybe it was because questioning came naturally in my work. Maybe it was because I was "too busy." Or maybe, just maybe, it was a form of procrastination. A way to avoid the truth that often comes when I slow down and actually listen.

That moment changed something. I began to build intentional inquiry into my life, especially in seasons of stress and growth. Because here's the truth: *When things get busy, curiosity is often the first thing to go.*

People default to reacting. They focus on checking boxes and finishing to-dos. They mistake motion for meaning. But leadership, real, impactful leadership, requires reflection.

TAKING INVENTORY

So I started small. Every year, around December 31st, I do an "annual inventory." It usually happens during our family vacation, far from the office, ideally in a cabin in the mountains. With some distance and space, I look back. I journal the highlights, the hard moments, the lessons, and the surprises.

I ask myself these questions:

- What were your biggest wins?
- What were your biggest losses?
- What obstacles got in the way of your success?
- What changed your mind this year?
- What brought you joy and energized you?
- What drained you or pulled you off course?
- What did fear stop you from doing?
- How will you overcome that next year?
- What will you do differently?

These aren't revolutionary, but they're *real*. They've helped me make better, more aligned decisions. They've made me a better leader.

Now, I don't wait for the end of the year. At the start of every quarter, I carve out thirty to sixty minutes to ask:

- How are your goals progressing?
- Are they still relevant?
- Do you need to redefine success?
- What's holding you back, and is it in your control?
- Are you chasing your vision or someone else's expectation?
- Where do you feel momentum?
- As a leader, have you made space for others to feel seen and heard?

- Where have you built trust? Where do you need to rebuild it?

- What feedback have you received (or avoided)?

This practice doesn't just shape my strategy. It sharpens my awareness. Getting better at asking questions of *others* starts with learning to ask them of *yourself*.

RITUALS OF CURIOSITY

You don't have to wait for a new year or new quarter to build this muscle.

- **Journal prompts**: Start or end your day with a single question.

- **Weekly reflection**: Ask, "What surprised me this week?" or "What did I avoid?"

- **The Questions Lens™ in meetings**: Start your staff meeting with a question. "What's one win you had this week?" "Where are you stuck?"

- **Family dinner check-ins**: "What's one thing you learned today?"

- **Sales debriefs**: "What did the client *not* say out loud?"

Questions don't need a big stage. They just need a moment. And a habit.

At work, we've started incorporating curiosity rituals:

- Kicking off client projects with open-ended, thought-provoking questions.

- Ending video shoots by asking, "What didn't we ask that we should have?"
- Using OSCARS as part of our debrief process.
- Sharing one "question of the week" on a team chat.

At home, we do something similar with our son. Before bed, we ask:

- What did you love about today?
- What did you learn today?
- What are you grateful for?

These tiny rituals build something bigger: a culture of inquiry. One that doesn't just value answers, but invites deeper understanding.

What Gets in the Way?

- **Impatience**: We want fast answers. Questions take time.
- **Control**: We think that truth will lead to less control.
- **Fear of the truth**: Sometimes, we already know the answer and it requires change.

But growth lives on the other side of the question. Always.

If you want to make this a true habit, here's a seven-day challenge. Each day, ask yourself:

1. What am I avoiding?

2. What's working and why?

3. What am I pretending not to know?

4. Where am I being reactive instead of intentional?

5. What feedback would help me grow right now?

6. What's one question I need to ask someone else today?

7. What truth is waiting to be revealed?

Repeat the challenge quarterly, monthly, or whenever you feel stuck.

If that's too much work, make it simple. Before you answer any question that's asked of you, respond with a question. Asking better questions isn't a box to check, it's a way of living. A practice. The more you practice it, the more your life and leadership will shift from busy to intentional, from reactive to curious, from stuck to evolving.

So go ahead. Ask like a leader.

NOTES

Note from Introduction

1. Ready, Lauren, dir. 2018. *You Must Believe: A LIFEline To Success*. Forever Ready Productions.

Notes from Chapter 1

2. Jeffrey Davis, "The Paradox of Expertise," *Psychology Today*, June 28, 2019, https://www.psychologytoday.com/us/blog/tracking-wonder/201906/the-paradox-expertise.

3. Malcolm Gladwell, *Outliers: The Story of Success* (New York: Little, Brown and Company, 2008), 42.

4. Philip E. Tetlock and Barbara A. Mellers, "The Paradox of Human Expertise: Why Experts Get It Wrong," in *Cambridge Handbook on Expertise and Expert Performance*, ed. K. Anders Ericsson, Neil Charness, Paul J. Feltovich, and Robert R. Hoffman (Cambridge: Cambridge University Press, 2011), 431–448.

5. Itiel E. Dror, "The Paradox of Human Expertise: Why Experts Get It Wrong," in The Paradoxical Brain, ed. Narinder Kapur (Cambridge: Cambridge University Press, 2011), 177–88.

Note from Chapter 2

6. Kenneth Savitsky, Nicholas Epley, and Boaz Keysar, "Is Closeness the Enemy of Communication?," *Journal of Experimental Social Psychology* 47, no. 1 (2011): 1–5, https://doi.org/10.1016/j.jesp.2010.09.002.

7. Savitsky, "Is Closeness the Enemy?"

Note from Chapter 4

8. Oliver Burkeman, *Meditations for Mortals* quoting Sheldon B. Kapp.

Note from Chapter 5

9. Declan Lowney, dir. 2020. *Ted Lasso* (Apple TV), Season 1, Episode 8.

Notes from Chapter 7

10. Pooja K. Agarwal, "Retrieval Practice and the Protective Effect of Elaborative Interrogation," *Perspectives on Psychological Science* 7, no. 6 (2012): 623–633, https://doi.org/10.1177/1529100612453266.

11. Amy C. Edmondson, *The Fearless Organization: Creating Psychological Safety in the Workplace for Learning, Innovation, and Growth* (Hoboken, NJ: Wiley, 2019).

Note from Chapter 10

12. Carl R. Rogers and Richard E. Farson, *Active Listening* (Chicago: Industrial Relations Center, University of Chicago, 1957), https://wholebeinginstitute.com/wp-content/uploads/Rogers_Farson_Active-Listening.pd

Note from Chapter 11

13. Jessica R. Andrews-Hanna, "The Brain's Default Network and Its Adaptive Role in Internal Mentation," *The Neuroscientist* 18, no. 3 (2012): 251–270.

Note from Chapter 12

14. Alvin W. Gouldner, "The Norm of Reciprocity: A Preliminary Statement," *American Sociological Review* 25, no. 2 (1960): 161–178.

ACKNOWLEDGMENTS

There are so many people who've helped me along the way in this book writing process.

Dr. Sarah Petschonek, thanks for purchasing my first copy through Venmo, long before it was even written. And scheduling writing sessions with me back when this was just a dream. You're always reminding me to "go for it!" and connecting dots I don't always see. Your friendship and guidance has been so encouraging.

Micheala Riley, thank you for being my lifelong best friend. You've always encouraged me and my crazy ideas. And along this book writing journey, you were always so encouraging that this message needed to be shared with the world. Also thank you for providing a beautiful mountain-like space for me to think, cold plunge, and enjoy nature with our families.

Sally Zimney, thanks for being my speaking coach and professional nudger. Your guidance on redefining my speaking topics helped me gain clarity to write this book—and as an author yourself, you inspired me to "just do it" instead of keeping it on my yearly goals list. Also thanks for introducing me to cold plunging, Marco Polo, and the mantra "they already don't like you!"

Katey Perkins, Nicki Storey, Natalie Linney, Mary Gunning, and Julie Hopkins, thanks for holding down the fort at Forever Ready Productions, letting me share these methods and stories, and continuing to do the work while I stepped away to write this book.

DeAndre Brown, thank you for your friendship and for trusting me and my team to tell your story. Your life's work inspires me everyday and I am grateful that you both allow me to share it with people all over the country and that you keep doing the work. You've changed me and I am so grateful that God brought you (and your family) into my life.

Lisa Anderson, thank you for your heart and your willingness to be the change in our world. You solve problems by doing the work and getting others to join alongside you. I think about it often and I am inspired by the faith that guides you through it all.

The Ready Brothers, Dan, Joe & Bob, thank you for playing your nerdy video games on Tuesday nights so that I could write. I know that's not why you play but it might be one thing in the world that I don't have FOMO about. I knew every Tuesday night, like clockwork, that I could dedicate time to this book without missing out on time with my husband.

The Ready Sisters (in-law), Sara, Mary & Jess, thank you for providing feedback on the book cover and helping me talk through this idea long before it was written.

The Readys, Laurie & Bob, thanks for brainstorming with me and supporting me as I brought this book into the world amidst some pretty unpredictable and chaotic moments in your life. I hope this book is a reminder of the hope we all believe in when we get curious about each other.

Allison Davis, thanks for reinforcing my internal thoughts and guiding me as I outlined, wrote, and began sharing this with the world.

Lori Turner-Wilson, thanks for encouraging me to write this book, being a sounding board when I felt discouraged, and allowing me to text you every time I hit a milestone—usually while I was in the mountains.

Amy Quale, thank you for helping me jump start writing this book. Being a part of your coaching cohort, nearly a year before I wrote this, helped me begin writing. If I hadn't spent four months with you, this book would still be a thought in my mind. I am inspired by the way you lean into your values and support authors in bringing their words to life and impacting the world.

Jenn Whitmer, thank you for always cheering for me. And walking the book writing journey with me too. Your constant reminder that two things can be true at the same time helped me get through the busiest and most stressful parts of writing this book. And your message of joy being deeply rooted in everything continues to inspire me.

Carrie Campbell, thank you for your friendship and encouragement. Your leadership inspires me and you've changed the way I think about what it means to recognize my team and thank people for their impact. You have been a light in my life and I am grateful that speaking brought us together.

John Salajka, thanks for being my business coach, encouraging my ideas, asking the right questions, and inspiring a chapter in this book. Your insight has helped me question limiting beliefs and become a better leader and person.

Trish Kendall, thank you for your friendship and encouragement. And for inspiring me to "make a first choice" in sitting down to commit to finishing writing the book. I am forever grateful that we met and that you planted the seed on the paradox of expertise.

Nancy Knous, thank you for being a friend and mentor who asks the right questions at the right time, especially the one inspired in a chapter in this book. I admire your faith and the way you lead with vision and values. Thank you for teaching me how to think differently about dreams and begin to live them.

Nick Gant, thank you for your friendship and business advice. And thanks for asking a question that inspired a chapter in this book and changed my routine. Making time to think has been one of the best things for my business and my dreams.

My Vistage Group, thank you to every member that's been a part of the group over the years. Your wisdom, questions and accountability are a big reason I've made it through some of the toughest days in my business. You've been there through it all and it's an honor to share moments with you too.

Dr. Mary "MJ" McConner, thank you for walking this book journey with me. Our writing sessions, conversations about how to incorporate stories into our tools, and overall encouragement has meant so much to me. I am grateful for your friendship and support. And for the message of inclusivity that you encourage and embody in everything you do.

Julie Long and Shannon Curtis, thanks for being my hype women. Whenever I talk about something crazy, you always cheer me on—and sometimes even schedule a girls' dinner to celebrate the idea. You remind me what it means to be in community.

My former colleagues at KCRG, KWWL, WOWT, and WMC, thanks for helping me understand the power of questions. We covered so many moments that shaped me—both good and hard. If you worked with me, you influenced me. Please know that I carry our experiences with me.

Craig Schaefer, thanks for being my Loras College advisor turned colleague and friend. You helped me frame storytelling through an ethical and mission-driven lens, and challenged me to tell stories that matter, learn a little bit about everything, and lead with faith.

Bobbi Earles, thanks for being a mentor and friend who always showed up—whether for coffee or wine. You knew how to ask great questions, listened to my answers, and shared just enough of yourself to make me reflect, stay curious, and want to make a bigger impact.

Chad Cannon, thank you for your words of wisdom shared on a panel in Nashville in April 2025. You may not know it but those words inspired me to take action and actually write the book, instead of wait. I barely know you … but your message resonated loud and clear.

Ryan Holiday, thanks for influencing me in one of my darkest leadership moments—even if you don't know it. Your books have helped me and so many fellow leaders think more deeply and lead more intentionally … starting with ourselves.

Mel Robbins, thank you for your message of taking action. You have been a constant voice in my head whenever things get hard. And your story of hard work and growth inspires me to keep going. We don't know each other ,but your impact is always being felt.

Spotify, thank you for your lo-fi beats playlists. They basically got me to focus and pay attention long enough to write this book. I am still waiting for them to show up on my yearly Spotify recap.

ABOUT LAUREN READY

Lauren Ready is an Emmy-winning filmmaker, keynote speaker, and storytelling strategist who helps leaders and organizations harness the power of questions to uncover stories, drive action, and deepen human connection.

She is the Founder and Principal Storyteller of Forever Ready Productions, a nationally recognized video production company founded in 2014 that has helped nonprofits raise over $18 million (and counting) through purpose-driven storytelling. A six-time Regional Emmy award winner, Lauren's work has changed laws, shaped campaigns, and sparked movements—most notably with her acclaimed short documentary *What We'll Never Know*, which led to a change in child interrogation laws in Tennessee.

She has been honored as the Memphis Business Journal's Small Business of the Year, a Super Woman in Business, and a Top 40 Under 40 leader. In 2024, she was named a Just Society

Awards Finalist by Evident Change for her contributions to criminal justice reform through storytelling.

Based in Memphis with her husband, Scott, and their son, Max, Lauren is also a certified drone pilot, among the less than 7 percent of women in the US with that credential, and an avid explorer committed to visiting every US National Park, camera in hand and curiosity leading the way.

BEFORE YOU GO...

Thank you for reading this book.

If something in these pages sparked a thought, shifted your mindset, or changed how you lead, I'd be so grateful if you'd take two minutes to leave a review.

Your feedback not only helps future readers decide to pick up the book, it helps me grow as an author, speaker, and storyteller.

Head to Amazon (or wherever you purchased the book) and share what stood out to you.

Was there a chapter you bookmarked?

A question you've already used in a conversation?

A story that stayed with you?

I read every single one.

Thanks for being curious about this work, and about what's possible.

Lauren